Becoming God's Change Agents

Becoming God's Change Agents

To Helen
If you find a chapter that
is just for you.

Jack Blanch

Jack Blanch

ISBN: 1537743503
ISBN 13: 9781537743509
Library of Congress Control Number: 2016915880
CreateSpace Independent Publishing Platform
North Charleston, South Carolina

Contents

Foreword

MANY SERIOUS FOLLOWERS of Jesus feel they do not measure up to the standards God has set for them.

"I need to read the Bible more."

"I need to witness more."

"I need to study the Bible more."

"I need to be more obedient to God."

"I need to get my spiritual act together."

Each of those statements is true for *some* believers. But almost without exception, believers will say, "I need to pray more." Everyone senses that need and will admit it.

However, "more prayer" may not be what is really needed. In reality, we need help in the "how," "what," "why," and "when" of prayer. In this marvelous guide, Jack Blanch goes to the heart of prayer and instructs us on its many elements. When you read this book, you do not feel chastised for lack of prayer but rather encouraged in understanding and receiving practical help on actually praying. It does not demand huge amounts of time praying but rather that we simply pray in the natural course of life.

As I read his manuscript, I thought, *This is written for me.* I needed it. I was challenged by Jack's personal struggles in learning to pray as well as by an abundance of examples and stories of prayer. What I appreciated most was the thorough citing of scripture to instruct and illustrate his teaching. This is a practical, realistic, down-to-earth guide. It centers prayer in God, not our efforts or piety. It shows God's great desire that we communicate with Him, far beyond the asking of personal requests.

I encourage you to read a chapter and then practice what it teaches. This is not a book to read in one sitting. Like so many classic works on prayer, it should be digested slowly with meditation…and, of course, with prayer.

Jerry E. White, PhD
Major General, USAF, Ret.
International President Emeritus, the Navigators

Acknowledgments

WE ARE FOREVER grateful to our team of intercessors from 1962 to the present, 2016. Most of you prayed faithfully at least three times a week, and some of you have said you prayed every day and continue to this day, for fifty-four years! Your reward in eternity will be great. Many people have come to Christ, and many have joined the forces of those leaving a legacy of disciple makers.

A goodly number have become church leaders, pastors, and missionaries, and they will rise up at the resurrection to call you blessed.

The original force of the two hundred dedicated prayers has grown over the years to seven hundred regular intercessors.

A special salute to the praying force from Melrose Baptist of Oakland; First Baptist of Spokane; Irvington Presbyterian of Irvington, California; Walnut Creek Presbyterian Church of California; First Christian Church of Los Gatos, California; College Avenue Baptist of San Diego; First Baptist of San Jose; Golden Hills Community Church of Brentwood; and Good Shepherd Church of Boring, Oregon.

Joann and I have been regularly carried upon these prayers by you who bore us up day after day during these years. Through your prayers, God has blessed us beyond measure and guarded us through many perils, physical and spiritual, and continues to bless and help us to this day.

One final tribute goes to my good friend, fellow missionary, and missions' statesman, Ken Williams, who is now with Jesus. He taught me in the beginning of our career to raise up this prayer force.

Jack Blanch
Colorado Springs

1

The Intercessor

HAVE YOU EVER felt helpless to affect the things that are going on around you? Have you felt the inability to help to affect the lives of family members, people outside of the Kingdom of God, the progress of the Great Commission, your city, your church, politics, or another nation? It doesn't have to be that way. God calls His people to become change agents. This comes through faith in His promises and an understanding of His purposes, His characteristics, and His desires.

You can be God's instrument to change people, cities, and nations. God desires to do this through anyone who would be God's man or woman of mercy, grace, love, and faith.

An intercessor is a person of compassion who stands between heaven and earth. With one hand, he or she holds the hand of God and with the other holds people, cities, and nations. Through the ages, God has called for intercessors in the fulfillment of His desires. God has said:

> The people of the land have practiced oppression and committed robbery, and they have wronged the poor and needy and have oppressed the sojourner without justice. I searched for a man among them who would build up the wall and stand in the gap before Me for the land, so that I would not destroy it; but I found no one. Ezekiel 22:29–30.

To be God's change agent, you must grab hold of His magnificent promises by believing them. He calls men and women to do this. He is "astonished" that we don't. "And He saw that there was no man, and was astonished that there was no one to intercede" Isaiah 59:16a.

To be intercessors, we must draw near to the heart of God. This is not too bold a desire. It is snuggling up to our Father. "Draw near to God and He will draw near to you." James 4:8.

God Himself beckons you to ask Him to activate His power by asking Him to do great and mighty things. How often have you passed over His beckoning? He has said: "Ask, and it will be given to you; seek, and you will find; knock, and it will be opened to you." Matthew 7:7.

Have you ever thought of these open promises in the light of His great purposes or only in the light of your needs?

If you start this amazing journey, it will be necessary that you change your focus from self to God the Father and Christ the Son. Focusing on self will only result in little dreams and small petitions. There is a man in the Bible about whom only two short verses are written. God put them there to inspire us to ask great things. This man did ask something for himself, but I don't think that necessarily means he was self-centered. The following is one of the two verses:

> Now Jabez called on the God of Israel, saying, "Oh that You would bless me indeed and enlarge my border, and that Your hand might be with me, and that You would keep *me* from harm that *it* may not pain me!" <u>And God granted him what he requested.</u> 1 Chronicles 4:10.

Would thinking on this verse inspire you in a new way to pray for yourself? Is it possible that God, after so many centuries, is still able and willing to grant people the desires of their hearts if their desires coincide with His? To ask is not enough. We must ask in His will with faith and with right motives.

- **We are to ask with the right motives.**
  God is very interested in why we ask him for things.

> You lust and do not have; *so* you commit murder. You are envious and cannot obtain; *so* you fight and quarrel. You do not have because you do not ask. You ask and do not receive, because you ask with wrong motives, so that you may spend *it* on your pleasures. James 4:2–3.

- **We are to ask seeking things that He wants.**

> This is the confidence which we have before Him, that, if we ask anything according to His will, He hears us. And if we know that He hears us *in* whatever we ask, we know that we have the requests which we have asked from Him.
> 1 John 5:14–15.

Effective praying is not really that complicated. It is asking with good reasons and with a heart that is submitted to God's purposes and desires. These ideas will be repeated over and over again in this book.

- **We are to ask in faith.**
  It is asking and believing. Faith must be mingled with our requests.

> "And all things you ask in prayer, believing, you will receive." Matthew 21:22.

Warning: choose your associates carefully.

We must be aware of the importance of the people we associate with. The people you choose to associate with will either inspire you to greater dreams or kill every new one.

Some years ago God gave me great promises and commissioned me to go to an unbelieving nation. When my wife and I got there, we found that other missionaries before us had labeled this nation as a graveyard for missionaries. They said that people like us would not last long and would return home defeated.

I recognized that if I was around them, they would kill my faith. I decided to avoid them, though we lived in the same city. It did not become our graveyard; it became a nation of great blessing to us and the people we reached. Choose your associates carefully.

The opportunity of your life stands before you. Will you let it slip away? Will you grasp it and change the eternal destiny of yourself and others? If you can grasp it today, your eternity and that of others will change forever. Start this eternal journey without delay.

Invite another to join you on this journey. Recruit a partner for big thinking, and stimulate each other. Don't keep the opportunity to yourself. Share it boldly.

Men and women, before you have boldly become world changers and are reaping the results, join that number without delay.

After committing yourself to becoming an intercessor, you may ask, "Where do I go from here?" The following chapters are meant to guide you in becoming a life changer and a world changer. But remember, you will become a colaborer with God, and He intends to guide you. Realizing this, we must start our journey by understanding His power, character, and purposes. The task of an intercessor is not to persuade God to do what the intercessor wants but rather to have the attitude of Jesus when He said, "Not my will but your will be done" and to seek to understand God and His purposes. It is asking according to His will that brings change in the name of Christ. We are to represent Him.

2

Helping the Intercessor Understand God's Power and Beauty

The initial step in becoming a change agent for God is to understand God in His power and the beauty of His person. Moses asked to see God's glory. In response God declared what He is like. In this chapter, we pursue comprehending His power and person so that when we ask, we are representing Him and what He wants.

- **Part I—Praying from an Understanding of His Power**
  The prophet Jeremiah understood that God's power was unlimited. And so, he wrote: "Ah Lord GOD! Behold, You have made the heavens and the earth by **Your great power** and by Your outstretched arm! Nothing is too difficult for You." Jeremiah 32:17.

This is what the men and women of old believed. God is looking for men and women of *this age* to see Him as El Elyon (God Most High). Do you remember how Abram took 318 of his servants plus the men whom three brothers, friends of Abram, could recruit, and that they pursued the armies of four kings and defeated them? It was an astounding victory by a very small army against four powerful kings. Upon returning from great victory, this happened:

> And Melchizedek king of Salem brought out bread and wine; now he was a priest of God Most High. He blessed him and said, "Blessed be Abram of God Most High, Possessor of heaven and earth; And blessed be **God Most High, who has delivered your enemies into your hand**." Genesis 14:18–20.

This was not a great accomplishment by Abram. It was a great accomplishment by God, according to Melchizedek.

The book of Hebrews, chapter 11, speaks of these men and women of faith. The writer reminds us that the power of God was displayed time and again throughout history. As the writer of Hebrews says, time would fail him to recount all the mighty acts of God through these men and women.

One of the individuals mentioned in Hebrews 11 is Gideon. Do you remember Gideon in Judges chapters 6–8? He had 32,000 warriors, and God directed him to reduce the army to 300 so that they would see how great the power of God was. The army that they went up against was enormous. In chapter 8 God says Gideon and his men killed 120,000 swordsmen. American casualties from the Vietnam War, men and women who valiantly sacrificed their lives are officially listed at 58,303. More than twice that number perished in the battle with Gideon! But this was not to display the might of Gideon but rather the might of God who enabled them to do this.

The power of God is not only displayed in great battles against overwhelming odds; it is also displayed in God's willingness to alter the natural course of our solar system. Consider the request of King Hezekiah and the responses of the prophet Isaiah and of God Himself:

> This shall be the sign to you from the LORD, that the LORD will do the thing that He has spoken: shall the shadow go forward ten steps or go back ten steps?
> So, Hezekiah answered, "It is easy for the shadow to decline ten steps; no, but let the shadow turn backward ten steps." Isaiah the prophet cried to the LORD, and He brought the shadow on the stairway

> back ten steps by which it had gone down on the stairway of Ahaz.
> 2 Kings 20:9–11.

The stairway of Ahaz served as a type of sundial. The renowned scholar Matthew Henry comments on this passage about the sun going backward and the light of day continuing longer than normal in response to prayer. Think about the enormity of how this act of God may have impacted our solar system.

We in this day do not live by the Old Testament but by the New Testament and the power of the risen Christ. But we should be inspired by the illustrations of the Old Testament and the great miracles of God that are clearly explained there. One of their purposes is to increase our faith and expectation for God to use His great power. "Now faith is the assurance of *things* hoped for, the conviction of things not seen. *For by it the men of old gained approval.*" Hebrews 11:1–2.

We need to see Jesus as the Mighty God who came to earth to walk among us and to do great acts among us. Here is a prophecy about Jesus:

> For a child will be born to us, a son will be given to us; And the government will rest on His shoulders; And His name will be called Wonderful Counselor, **Mighty God**, Eternal Father, Prince of Peace.
> Isaiah 9:6.

As Jesus (God) lived among us, His power and authority amazed that generation. Let's look at just one illustration of an act of Jesus and His teaching.

> Which is easier, to say, 'Your sins are forgiven,' or to say, 'Get up, and walk'? But so that you may know that the Son of Man has authority on earth to forgive sins—then He said to the paralytic, 'Get up, pick up your bed and go home.' And he got up and went home. But when the crowds saw *this*, **they were awestruck**, and glorified God, who had given such authority to men.
> Matthew 9:5–8.

They saw the healing power of Jesus but also heard him explain the far greater miracle: the power to forgive sins! **They were awestruck!**

Have we lost the sense of being awestruck? Consider the immensity of a single conversion, for example, your own. Were all of your sins washed away with the blood of Jesus? Did you get a whole new heart sensitive to follow God? Does the Holy Spirit reside in you to guide and to empower you day by day? Have you become desensitized over time to these miracles? Can you still become awestruck over them?

My wife and I have seen this new spiritual birth many, many times, and it never loses its power to amaze us. Maybe you have never helped someone to faith in Christ. If you have not, ask God for this immense privilege within the next year. The new birth is permanent, and we often have contact with people who we have led to Christ. People who came to Christ forty years ago through our ministry, express to us their profound gratitude to God for being saved eternally and for His presence in their lives every day and for the transformation He has wrought. They continue to be awestruck by the enormity of it—and not just awestruck, but with a deep gratitude to God for their eternal position in Him.

A few days ago, I attended the funeral for my brother who had passed away suddenly. He had dedicated his life over the past few years to working in the Texas prison system to bring Christ to the inmates. He also used his home as a halfway house for believers who had served their time.

After the service, I walked around, meeting people who had come. I met a tall young man who had lived with my brother for over a year after leaving prison. He was a new man in Christ.

I also saw a beautiful young mother seated with her two- or three-year-old daughter in her lap. I knelt down in front of her to hear her story. She was not sobbing, but tears were streaming from one eye down alongside her nose and onto her blouse. Her little daughter, snuggled against her, was watching her mother. That young man I had seen was her husband. My brother had helped him to a new life and both of them to a new marriage. They were living "awestruck." I beg you to not lose being awestruck with God and how He transforms people.

God's power and authority are unlimited, but the intercessor must understand that He has set parameters and conditions as to how and when He uses this power.

For example, He has the power and authority to end Satan's rebellion and opposition to Him. However, in His wisdom, He has decided that this is not the time to exercise this power but rather to keep it under restraint.

The most common complaint that I hear from nonbelievers about God is His use of His power. They ask, "Why He does not end all suffering *now*?" The second question seems to be, "Why does He permit injustice? Why not stop it *now* if He has the authority?"

Even very religious people are puzzled by God's restraint. At the crucifixion of Jesus, they addressed Jesus as He hung on the cross and said: "He saved others; He cannot save Himself. He is the King of Israel; let Him **now** come down from the cross, and we will believe in Him." Matthew 27:42.

If we are to pray correctly, we must understand in some measure the wisdom of God and the timing of God.

Immerse Yourself in a Different Environment

If we are going to *be men and women of God in this age*, we must live outside of the thought patterns of the materialistic and naturalistic environment in which we live. But where will we get that new environment? We must return to the events of the Gospels and of Acts. This is the God-conscious environment that the apostles lived in. Soak yourself in that environment, reading those books over and over again—although I don't mean by this to exclude or minimize the rest of the New Testament or of the Bible.

Because of the naturalistic environment that we live in, many believers are reluctant to talk about the God of miracles. They seem to have accepted a naturalistic God who created the world and then sat down to watch. In their minds He heals only by doctors, medications, and health foods. We must return to the *faith* of the New Testament and its supernatural environment. We must live in the environment of the apostles. Here is just one short illustration of that environment:

> At Lystra a man was sitting who had no strength in his feet, lame from his mother's womb, who had never walked. This man was listening to Paul as he spoke, who, when he [Paul] had fixed his gaze on him <u>and had seen that he had faith to be made well</u>, said with a loud voice, "Stand upright on your feet." And he leaped up and *began* to walk. Acts 14:8–10.

Have you ceased to believe in the God who does the miraculous, both great and small? If we want to expect God to do great things through our prayers, we will need to live daily with an expectant spirit that God can do great things in and through our lives. We also must look to see the hand of God in our circumstances, not attributing everything to natural causes.

This week, while I was talking with a new believer who has lived immersed in this naturalistic environment, he said God had done many things that at the time he did not recognize as from God. Now he is starting to see things differently. Five years ago he had a foot operation that was not healing. His doctor recommended a special way of bandaging that required a daily changing and some expertise. He was not doing it very well at home. A female acquaintance said she had gone through some nurse training, and this was a specialty that she had learned. She then changed his bandages daily for him until the wound was healed. Now he sees her as a godsend although, at the time, he saw her only as a chance happening.

We all face daily difficulties. It is not the absence of difficulties that evidences the power of God; it is His presence in the midst of them!

Last month my wife, Joann, awoke from sleep, unable to stand because the pain in one knee was excruciating. At 6:00 p.m., I took her to the emergency room for x-rays. After taking them, the doctor could not get a radiologist to read them. Finally, at midnight, Joann dressed, and I took her home without a diagnosis. The nurses and doctor were totally embarrassed at their inability to get the x-rays read.

The next morning I called the hospital to see if the x-rays had been read and what the diagnosis was. This was a Saturday morning. Can you imagine who answered the phone? Not the regular phone operator, *but the x-ray technician who had taken Joann's x-rays the night before*! She understood the whole situation and immediately arranged to personally give me the CD of the x-rays and a written diagnosis of them. Can you see a miracle here? Someone has said that our extremity is God's opportunity. How easily, it seems, that we often attribute what God has done to naturalism.

I encouraged you to soak yourselves in the Gospels and Acts to change your environmental bias. This week while reading the Gospel of Matthew, I was astounded by John the Baptist's perspective of the supernatural. Pharisees and Sadducees were coming to him, but not in the spirit of repentance, and he called them vipers. But what astounds me is what he believed God could do:

> And do not suppose that you can say to yourselves, "We have Abraham for our father"; for I say to you that *from these stones* God is able to raise up children to Abraham. Matthew 3:9.

He believed that God had such power that He could turn a rock into a man or woman of faith!

Are people around you rock hard? Live in the spiritual environment of John the Baptist and expect God to turn a heart of stone into a throbbing heart of flesh. Would you believe that God has promised to do this in our times?

> Moreover, I will give you a new heart and put a new spirit within you; and I will remove the heart of stone from your flesh and give you a heart of flesh.
> Ezekiel 36:26.

Think a moment about your environment and your expectations from God. What have you been expecting Him to do? Are you living expecting God to do unusual things? Possibly you have been asking God to make things just a little better rather than to bring total transformation.

Review your prayers of this past week. How would you classify them? Are you praying for transformation or for just a little bit of modification?

The Apostle Paul lived in the realm of the supernatural. He expected God to perform according to His power and love. Here is how he prayed for others:

> For this reason I bow my knees before the Father, from whom every family in heaven and on earth derives its name, that He would grant you, according to the riches of His glory, to be strengthened with power through His Spirit in the inner man, so that Christ may dwell in your hearts through faith; *and* that you, being rooted and grounded in love, may be able to comprehend with all the saints what is the breadth and length and height and depth, and to know the love of Christ which surpasses knowledge, that you may be filled up to all the fullness of God. Ephesians 3:14–19.

Have you ever prayed for yourself, your spouse, and others that they would be filled with all the fullness of God? There are other men and women of *this age* who are praying that way. Join these men and women who dare to pray for their families what Paul prayed for the Ephesian church. When I became a new believer, others taught me to pray this way, and they prayed this way for me.

Review the prayer above in its entirety. If you cannot pray that way for people, then begin praying to God to raise your faith to this level.

After Paul prayed these things, he then made the astounding comment in the next verse: "Now to **Him who is able to do** far more abundantly beyond all that we ask or think, according to the power that works within us." Ephesians 3:20.

One day a rich man came to Jesus and asked, "Teacher, what good thing shall I do that I may obtain eternal life?" Matthew 19:16. The answer was too difficult for him, and he walked away grieving. The disciples were there listening and were deeply touched, seeing the man and listening to Jesus.

> Again I say to you, it is easier for a camel to go through the eye of a needle, than for a rich man to enter the kingdom of God." When the

> disciples heard *this*, they were very astonished and said, "Then who can be saved?" And looking at *them* Jesus said to them, "With people this is impossible, but with God all things are possible."
> Matthew 19:24–26.

- **Part II—Praying from an Understanding of the Beauty of God**

Seeing His great power is a good motivator. But there are other characteristics of God that also encourage us to believe in Him for great things.

Every aspect of God affects our ability to pray with faith. Some other aspects of God especially encourage us to believe that God will reach out to people.

The following qualities are like beautiful jewel adornments on a lady who is already beautiful in herself. These qualities are like rubies, emeralds, opals, pearls, and diamonds. Each one presents an aspect of the attractiveness of Christ and God.

His Patience Is Beautiful

Some wonder why God is delaying so long in sending Christ back for His second coming. One aspect of the beauty of His patience is His desire that multitudes should be given time to repent and experience eternity with Christ.

> The Lord is not slow about His promise, as some count slowness, but is patient toward you, not wishing for any to perish but for all to come to repentance.
> 2 Peter 3:9.

About twenty years ago, I read that historians, as they attempted to calculate the total number of people who had lived on the earth, came to the conclusion that, because of the population explosion, *90 percent of the people who had ever lived on the earth were alive at that date*! Because of wars and sickness, the population of the earth grew very slowly until the population explosion that has been occurring during our lifetime. Think of that! The great majority of people who have ever lived throughout all time are alive now. Because Christ has delayed His coming, millions have entered the Kingdom of God during our lifetime. The patience of God has greatly multiplied the number of sons and daughters of God that will live in eternity. That is an expression of the beauty of His nature. And so Peter in that chapter concluded, "Regard the patience of our Lord as salvation."

As we go through life, God's patience becomes more and more valuable to us. In our immaturity we seem to see impatience as a virtue. As I mentioned in the thoughts about His power, we want to see Him use it *now*. We are prone to want Him to be patient with us but not with others, especially those whom we see as doing wrong. We seem to be saying, "God, be patient with me but not with my neighbor."

In Matthew 18 Jesus and Peter talk about forgiveness. Peter wants to know how much forgiveness he should offer to an offender. Jesus then compares the king of heaven, or God, to an earthly king and earthly debts. In this parable, a servant of the earthly king owed him 10,000 talents; it was probably either silver or gold. It is not specified because it does not make any difference. A talent weighed seventy-five pounds. The debt was equivalent to 375 *tons* of gold or silver! Probably no one on earth could come up with that amount of money. Jesus chooses an impossible debt as an illustration of what our sins would cost. The servant said to him, "Have patience with me, and I will repay you everything." It would take him an eternity to repay. "Have patience."

What is Jesus teaching? He is teaching of the limitless forgiveness of God and His patience with us. "And the lord of that slave felt compassion and released him and forgave him the debt." Matthew 18:27. The patience of God allows time for our development. "The farmer waits for the precious produce of the soil, being patient about it, until it gets the early and late rains." James 5:7. In His patience with us, we also learn forgiveness. Peter was having trouble with that. The second part of this illustration of forgiveness warns us against not offering it to others. He reveals that the forgiven servant did not take it to heart and treated with cruelty someone who owed him a small amount.

In my twenties and thirties, I did not feel I needed God's patience. I was doing fine, I thought. Now, in my eighties, I am so grateful for God's patience with me while I was in my twenties. At that time I could not see my needs. Now things are becoming clearer. As we grow we begin to see how weighty our sins are and how impossible it is to pay their price.

I am sure that I have no idea of the depth of my sins. But God was so patient with me in my blindness all those years, and even also to this day. How valuable is the patience of God to you? What price would you put on it? The patience of God is an indicator of the compassion and mercy of God. Next, we will consider the compassion and mercy of the Lord.

His Compassion Is Beautiful

> You have heard of the endurance of Job and have seen the outcome of the Lord's dealings that **the Lord is full of compassion and *is* merciful**. James 5:11.

These jewels are seen for their beauty in our personal encounters with the Lord. The appreciation of their value develops with each encounter.

As Moses walked with God in the desert, one day he begged God to show him His glory—in reality, the beauty of God. You will find this in Exodus 34. The Lord granted him his request and declared the great jewels of His nature.

> Then the LORD passed by in front of him and proclaimed, "The LORD, the LORD God, compassionate and gracious, slow to anger, and abounding in loving kindness and truth." Exodus 34:6.

How is compassion beautiful? Jesus expressed it in a parable that we could all understand: the parable of the Prodigal Son. Reading the entire parable in Luke 15 would give you the setting of gold for this jewel. It shows us how the Prodigal Son took his portion of his father's wealth and wasted it *all* on what we would say was wine, women, and song. He became deeply poverty-stricken. He came to the point of starvation and decided to return to his father who was still wealthy.

> So, he got up and came to his father. But while he was still a long way off, his father saw him and **felt compassion *for him***, and ran and embraced him and kissed him. Luke 15:20.

To someone who has received compassion, it is beautiful. God possibly had compassion on you and rescued you from all of your sins or from some terrible degradation that you brought upon yourself. What a beautiful characteristic. But be careful; to someone who has never received it or who feels no need for compassion, it is ugly and unjust!

How can this quality of compassion be seen as ugly? Look at the elder brother and his reaction.

> He became angry and was not willing to go in [to the feast]; and his father came out and *began* pleading with him…but the elder son said: "When this son of yours came, who has devoured your wealth with prostitutes; you killed the fattened calf for him." Luke 15:28–30.

To him the action of the father was inexcusable; it was not a jewel in his character but an ugly flaw.

Some people hate God or are deeply angered by His compassion to others, and some love God for His compassion. Compassion needs to be experienced to be appreciated.

As the subject of this book is intercession, I find that meditating on God's compassion helps me to pray for people with faith. Knowing that God is deeply touched by their situation enables me to connect with God and His feelings for the lost or for the saved in deep trouble. I can pray believing that He really wants to help them.

James, the author of that little book in the New Testament named after him, reminds us how to trust in these characteristics of God in His dealings with humans.

> We count those blessed who endured. You have heard of the endurance of Job and have seen the outcome of the Lord's dealings, that the Lord is full of compassion and *is* merciful. James 5:11.

His Graciousness Is Beautiful

I think that in the context of the above verse, this means that God is full of grace.

It can be said that mercy does not give to someone what he or she deserves; it withholds judgment. But grace gives to someone what he or she doesn't deserve; it pours out benefit to the undeserving. In the parable of the Prodigal Son, the father gives mercy in that he does not reprove the son for his wayward way. He also gives grace in that he bestows on the son a ring, a robe, and a kind reception. Mercy withholds judgments; grace gives benefits.

Part of the beauty of God is that His nature is to give. There is no end to His resource so He can give and give and continue giving.

> But if any of you lacks wisdom, let him ask of God, who gives to all generously and without reproach, and it will be given to him. But he must ask in faith.
> James 1:5–6.

For those who don't see the beauty of Christ's graciousness, they think that they must offer to God some merit of their own before He will give lavishly. Their prayers and expectations are based on merit. They understand nothing of grace. They expect little because they have not performed greatly. The person who expects great things from God is one who sets himself or herself aside and has focus only on the Giver and His resource. Are you poverty-stricken spiritually? Possibly you are expecting from God what you think you deserve. By this you take away God's beauty and establish your own. Can you ask great things just because God is great? God counsels you to open your mouth wide without self-consideration.

> I, the LORD, am your God, who brought you up from the land of Egypt; Open your mouth wide and I will fill it. Psalm 81:10.

Someone recently said that he did not want to expect big things from God because if those things did not happen, he would be disappointed. He thought that he would be setting himself up for a sense of failure. In this person's mind, God gives on the basis of one's performance. His idea was that the way to feel good about yourself is by attempting little and expecting little. The Apostle Paul had the opposite concept:

> Now to Him who is able to do far more abundantly beyond all that we ask or think, according to the power that works within us. Ephesians 3:20.

As I plead to God for help for people or cities or nations, I depend on these characteristics of God.

One could take each one of the many characteristics of God and realize the beauty of them. Meditate on each, and come to see their attractiveness.

His Mercy Is Beautiful

> We count those blessed who endured. You have heard of the endurance of Job and have seen the outcome of the Lord's dealings, **that the Lord is full of compassion and *is* merciful.** James 5:11.

I said earlier that it can be said that **mercy does not give** to someone what he or she deserves. It withholds judgment. Grace gives to someone what he or she doesn't deserve; it pours out benefit to the undeserving.

What kind of mercy has God given to me, I ask myself?

> For He who said, "DO NOT COMMIT ADULTERY," also said, "DO NOT COMMIT MURDER." Now if you do not commit adultery, but do commit murder, you have become a transgressor of the law. So speak and so act as those who are to be judged by *the* law of liberty. For judgment *will be* merciless to one who has shown no mercy; **mercy triumphs over judgment**. James 2:11–13.

The phrase "**mercy triumphs over judgment**" leaves a wonderful impression in my heart. There is something greater than the judgment of God; it is the mercy of God! How beautiful it is. The beauty of mercy embraces our soul and brings great joy to us. There is no condemnation that can triumph over mercy. I have meditated much in regard to my own life over the two great commandments of the Old Testament. About this a lawyer of religion proposed a question to Jesus:

> One of them, a lawyer, asked Him *a question*, testing Him, "Teacher, which is the great commandment in the Law?" And He said to him, 'YOU SHALL LOVE THE LORD YOUR GOD WITH ALL YOUR HEART, AND WITH ALL YOUR SOUL, AND WITH ALL YOUR MIND.' This is the great and foremost commandment. The second is like it, 'YOU SHALL LOVE YOUR NEIGHBOR AS YOURSELF.' **On these two commandments depend the whole Law and the Prophets**. Matthew 22:35–40.

What could be more important than the two thoughts that are the most important in the entire Old Testament? They sum up everything that God asked of people in those days.

I set myself to examine my life in the light of these two commands from God:

1. To love God with all my heart, soul, and mind.
2. To love my neighbor as myself.

This was a painful exercise for one who had a pretty good impression of himself.

First, I considered "all my heart," and I asked myself if I had ever, for one whole day, loved God with my entire heart. My sincere self-introspection caused me to conclude that never for an entire day in my life had I done this. Possibly for a few minutes of one day this had been true.

Then I asked about my soul. What is the soul? I thought it must be the center of my desires. I proposed to myself the same question. Had I ever for one whole day loved God with my entire soul? I concluded that no, not for one entire day had I ever done this.

How about my mind? Had I ever loved God with my whole thought process for one entire day? A solid no was the conclusion.

I concluded that not one day of my entire life had I kept the most important command of the entire Old Testament.

Next, I considered the second most important command of God, to love my neighbor as myself. How painful to consider my own selfishness. Yes, I had done things for others, but had that risen to the level of what I would do for myself? Not nearly. How did I do considering this question for one entire day of my life? Had I ever, all day long, or even a good part of one day, loved my neighbor as myself? I think not.

As I evaluated these two most important commandments of God, I concluded that every day of my life, I had broken both of these most important commandments. I deserved condemnation from God for my disobedience to God *every day of my life*. Oh, how I need mercy!

> He has showed you, O man, what is good. And what does the LORD require of you? To act justly and to love mercy and to walk humbly with your God.
> Micah 6:8 (NIV).

As I consider the failure of my life to live up to God's commandments, it produces a deep desire for mercy and causes me to walk humbly with my God. And oh, how I love that "**mercy triumphs over judgment**."

Is God beautiful or what?

What does this chapter mean for the intercessor, the one who is God's instrument to change people, cities, and nations? He has the power and desire to save the lost and to transform the believers, the ones who are His sons and daughters.

> Again I say to you, it is easier for a camel to go through the eye of a needle, than for a rich man to enter the kingdom of God. When the disciples heard *this*, they were very astonished and said, "**Then who can be saved?**" And looking at *them* Jesus said to them, "With people this is impossible, but with God all things are possible." Matthew 19:24–26.

This is our question as intercessors: **"Then who can be saved?"** We wrestle with this question. Jesus clarifies for us as well as for the apostles that this is not a work that humans can do but that we should not lose heart. It is a work that God can do. "With people this is impossible, but with God all things are possible."

This question not only applies to salvation but also to transformation of believers. **"Who then can be transformed?"** The answer to it is the same: "With people this is impossible, but with God all things are possible."

One day, Jesus let Peter know that he was going to fail:

> But I have prayed for you, that your faith may not fail; and you, when once you have turned again, strengthen your brothers. Luke 22:32.

Observe the confidence of Jesus: "*when* you have turned again," not "*if* you turn again."

God not only has the power to transform people, cities, and nations. Because of the beauty of His character, He also is moved to listen and answer our cries for help. Each of the characteristics that we have mentioned in this chapter moves us to believe that God will do things according to these characteristics.

In Matthew chapter 9, we read:

> Seeing the people, **He felt compassion for them**, because they were distressed and dispirited like sheep without a shepherd. Matthew 9:36.

This compassion was not without resolve and help. He asked the disciples to pray for more laborer shepherds for the people. Jesus, in His earthly body, was at one place in one moment of time. The people were all over—thousands of them in hundreds of cities in Israel. A multitude of the right kind of laborers is needed. There are many needy places in the world. God will burden each of us for different places.

Someone called me this week to say that he had *not been* praying for the people who I was informing him and others about to pray for. God had spoken to him to start praying. He intended to be obedient to that calling and wanted to let me know. Praise God!

The next day I was having coffee with a man in his seventies and speaking to him about faith in Christ. His openness was exceptional. He expressed amazement at some facets of the Gospel. Was this unusual openness a result of the prayers of the man who called me? I had told my caller that if God was putting this on his heart, he should expect fruit from his payers. I believe this fruit manifested itself the very next day. The compassion of Christ calls intercessors to pray with faith.

I often am touched by the mercy of Christ in such a way that it encourages me to pray with faith for believers who are doing terrible things. God does not "cross them off." His mercy reaches out to them. Immerse yourself in the life of Jesus. He will change your attitude. This past week a believer called me to inform me that the leaders of his church were threatening members of the congregation with fire from heaven if they resisted the will of the leaders. Even the Apostles James and John thought this way on one occasion:

> But they did not receive Him [Jesus], because He was traveling toward Jerusalem. When His disciples James and John saw *this*, they said, "Lord, do You want us to command fire to come down from

> heaven and consume them?" But He turned and rebuked them, and said, "You do not know what kind of spirit you are of; for the Son of Man did not come to destroy men's lives, but to save them." And they went on to another village. Luke 9:53–56.

What was the spirit that they were missing? It was the spirit of mercy. Knowing God's spirit of mercy should drive us to pray for God's blessing in these lives.

> But I say to you, love your enemies and pray for those who persecute you. Matthew 5:44.

These characteristics should be great motivators as we pray.

THE BEAUTY OF HIS LOVE

Love is the climax of everything. Life without love is cold and calculating. Love defies analysis. If I ask why God loves me, there is no answer. Love just is. Why do a mother and father love their newborn child? Don't try to answer that; you get into absurdities.

We have some statements from God. Without these statements, we would not know He loves us. Observation would not reveal this to us, only revelation. Observe the beauty of the flowers, animals, and birds. Then observe the creatures that eat the flowers, that kill the animals, that munch on the trees. For every beautiful thing, there is a corresponding destroyer of that beauty. God made them both. Observation of the creation will not lead you to believe that God is love.

God declares He has love and then demonstrates the reality of this love. Values express love or the absence of it. What would you give in exchange for your son or daughter or spouse? What would you refuse to give for them? Your love is defined by your response.

In the same way, God's love is defined by His response, His revelation of His values. What would He give for you or withhold?

How could we have known God's love without His placing a value on us? If we were in need, what would He refuse to give up for us that expresses how much He values us? He has declared and demonstrated that there is no limit that He will go to for us.

This is out beyond our human perception. God reveals to us that Jesus was in agreement with His Father to abandon the perfection of His heavenly abode to be born as a human, live in the womb of Mary, and then be born on Earth in our likeness. He not only traded heaven for Earth but also traded perfection and marvelous powers to become a human with its many limitations. God reveals that He "emptied Himself" to do this. Not only did Jesus demonstrate his value for people by doing this, but also the Father was willing to empty heaven of His son for a period of time, to have him absent from His presence and heavenly fellowship to demonstrate His love for us. "He who did not spare His own Son, but delivered Him over for us all, how will He not also with Him freely give us all things?" Romans 8:32. God declares to us that there is no limit that His love will not go to for us.

Then, of course, the cross is incomprehensible and foolishness to the human mind. How could the human birth and the cross be necessary for us? Surely there must have been a less expensive way for God to demonstrate His love for us. The price seems out of proportion to what it cost Him to rescue us from ourselves. If this was necessary, sin becomes exceedingly sinful.

God and Jesus so valued us that it was revealed that they were "pleased" for this great sacrifice. They had concluded that there was no other way. Love was demonstrated to the hilt.

The cross is the eternal symbol of the depth of the love of God. Jesus himself will bear for us the eternal symbol of his sacrifice in the cross by the signs of his love displayed in his resurrected body, by the holes in his hands, and by the slice made in his side by the Roman sword.

> But Thomas, one of the twelve, called Didymus, was not with them when Jesus came. So the other disciples were saying to him, "We have

> seen the Lord!" But he said to them, "Unless I see in His hands the imprint of the nails, and put my finger into the place of the nails, and put my hand into His side, I will not believe."
> After eight days His disciples were again inside, and Thomas with them. Jesus came, the doors having been shut, and stood in their midst and said, "Peace *be* with you."
> Then He said to Thomas, "Reach here with your finger, and see My hands; and reach here your hand and put it into My side; and do not be unbelieving, but believing." John 20:24–27.

This evidences the depth of the love of God. But there are more dimensions to the love of God.

> *And that you, being rooted and grounded in love, may be able to comprehend with all the saints what is the breadth and length and height and depth, and to know the love of Christ which surpasses knowledge, that you may be filled up to all the fullness of God. Ephesians 3:17–19.*

Could the "breadth" of God's love be so wide that it includes all of humanity? Could the "length" of his love be eternity? Could the "height" be reaching to the highest heavens? Whatever the dimensions are, we will not fully comprehend them until we reach our eternal home.

In summary, how does understanding God's power and beauty impact intercession? If you are convinced of His unlimited power, you realize that there is no request too big. Also, knowing that His other characteristics are unlimited, such as His love, compassion, and mercy, you know that there is no person on the globe who is outside of His interest or reach. None is so far away from God or so lost that He cannot reach him or her. Ask according to God's capacity and heart. Let your faith expand to the largeness of God.

> *My dear Father, I thank You that You will teach us about Yourself. Unless You were to teach us, what could we know? I am helpless to understand You*

unless You reveal Yourself to me and to us; the Eternal, the Unchangeable, the Father. You are My Father but also Our Father. Your power and beauty are displayed all around us all of the time, but we seem to be so blinded. Please lift the veil that is over Yourself. Help us not to be simply curiosity seekers but to be able to stand in awe of what You reveal, and to be brought to worship You in a new, intimate way. I thank You for what You will reveal, dear Father. Amen.

3

The Interaction between God and Humans

The intercessor's authority to bring about change.
"If you ask Me anything in My name, I will do *it*."—Jesus, John 14:14.

To be able to intercede with confidence and faith, we must understand the joy of being listened to by God. We must believe that He actually will change circumstances and people as He listens to our heartfelt petitions. He *delights* in responding. He tries to stir us up with hope and anticipation. He knows how bound we are by our physical limitations and surroundings. He desires that we break out of our little thinking, our earthly bound thinking.

As we read the Gospels, we are impressed with how often Jesus is working on breaking the disciples out of the human limitation of thinking. He knows that if we can perceive that we are colaborers with God, whole new horizons will open up to us. We will learn that we can soar with Him.

On the last night of His time here in an earthly body, He gave soaring promises and hope to the eleven by six different statements of unlimited prayer promises. When He spoke in John 16:24, He once again tried to lift them into another realm. "Until now you have asked for nothing in My name; ask and you will receive, so that your joy may be made full." He inspires them with "full joy." Think about that. He wants us to expect that kind of joy as we anticipate answers to prayers in His Name.

We were **created to rule. Rulers are given authority to make decisions.**

Part of this great expectation will come as we realize the exalted position He has given to His children. Yes, we are His servants, but His servants to rule in His Name. Let's consider first of all Genesis chapter 1 when He first creates humans.

Because God created us, He is very aware of our feelings, ideas, and needs. He deliberately gave us these needs and intends to use them to achieve His purposes.

It seems that two of the needs of humans are to be useful and creative. Before He even created humans, He decided that humans should rule over all moving things. Adam and Eve were not meant to be just two humans wandering the earth wondering what life in earth is all about.

God made Adam and Eve to be rulers over His own creation.

> Then God said, Let Us make man in Our image, according to Our likeness; and **let them rule** over the fish of the sea and over the birds of the sky and over the cattle and over all the earth, and over every creeping thing that creeps on the earth. Genesis 1:26.

So God did what He had proposed to do. He made them in His own image and then commanded Adam and Eve to be rulers over all living things on the earth.

> Be fruitful and multiply, and fill the earth, and subdue it; and **rule over** the fish of the sea and over the birds of the sky and over every living thing that moves on the earth. Genesis 1:28.

As rulers over all living things on the earth, God gave Adam and Eve authority and responsibility. He gave to them decision-making responsibility. Rulers must make decisions. That is part of their purpose.

This idea is continued in the New Testament. There we learn about believers being raised to a ruling status now and, in the future, heavenly life. We have been destined to rule.

> When Jesus rose from the dead, the Father seated him at His right hand: Which He brought about in Christ, when He raised Him from the dead and **seated Him at His right hand in the heavenly *places*.** Ephesians 1:20.

Then in Ephesians, Paul tells us that *we are seated* with Jesus in the heavenly places.

> But God, being rich in mercy, **because of His great love with which He loved us**, even when we were dead in our transgressions, made us alive together with Christ (by grace you have been saved), and raised us up with Him, **and seated us with Him in the heavenly *places* in Christ Jesus**. Ephesians 2:4–6.

Please take note that this is our present heavenly position, not a future one. But as we think about the future, that is our position then also.

> If we endure, **we will also reign with Him**. 2 Timothy 2:12.

The Word of God goes on to teach us that during Christ's millennial reign, we will be reigning with Him.

> You have made them *to be* a kingdom and priests to our God; **and they will reign upon the earth**. Revelation 5:10.

> Blessed and holy is the one who has a part in the first resurrection; over these the second death has no power, but they will be priests of

> God and of Christ **and will reign with Him for a thousand years.** Revelation 20:6.

But the Word of God goes on to say that this position of reigning will become eternal; we will reign forever and ever. In this position we are set above the angels and will be the ones to judge them for their errors.

> And there will no longer be *any* night; and they will not have need of the light of a lamp nor the light of the sun, because the Lord God will illumine them; **and they will reign forever and ever.** Revelation 22:5.

> Or do you not know that the saints will judge the world? If the world is judged by you, are you not competent *to constitute* the smallest law courts? Do you not know that we will judge angels? How much more matters of this life? 1 Corinthians 6:2–3.

The Sovereignty of God

What is the significance of the statement that God gives humans authority and responsibility, that He gives him decision-making responsibility? It modifies our understanding of the term "sovereign." We often hear the statement that God is sovereign. By that, some people imply that God makes all the decisions, but it is evident that God, in Genesis, delegates some decision making to Adam. God, who made the birds and beasts, defers to Adam, who names them.

> Out of the ground the LORD God formed every beast of the field and every bird of the sky, and brought *them* **to the man to see what he would call them.** Genesis 2:19.

God gave him a task and then did not overrule him by saying that He did not like Adam's choice of names. The Word of God says, **"And whatever the man called a living creature that was its name."** Genesis 2:19. Why do I point this out? Because some have been taught that God, being sovereign, make all the decisions, but you can see that right from the beginning of humanity, this was not the case.

Let me state clearly that God is sovereign.

The question is, what does "sovereign" mean?

Webster's Dictionary says this: "A monarch or other supreme ruler. A person who has sovereign power or authority."

The Bible calls God by this term. "He who is the blessed and only Sovereign, the King of kings and Lord of lords" 1 Timothy 6:15. Sovereign in the Greek means "ruler or potentate."

It seems that God is the ultimate ruler but not the only ruler. He is the "King *of* kings." He commissions others to rule under Him. When we say, God is sovereign, we should understand it means that He is the ultimate decision maker but not the only decision maker. An example of this would be the Roman Empire. Caesar was the supreme ruler, but he appointed kings to rule under him and for him. They were given authority to make decisions over the country they ruled. As Caesar could overrule a subordinate king, in a similar manner, if necessary, God can overrule a decision but may decide not to. In the case of Adam naming the animals, God accepted Adam's decisions.

God highly respects our decisions. He can override them but does not necessarily do that. His is not a false openness, one of just appearances. I read a book by one well-known theologian who stated that God wants us to ask because He loves to hear from us but has already decided what we can and can't have, so nothing will change. This theologian thought that God just wanted to hear from us, nothing more; the path was already set in concrete. In his viewpoint, there could be no changes. From this theologian's viewpoint, the idea of a petition was fine, but there would be no change.

I feel bad for those who take his viewpoint because they will see their petitions as useless, thinking that God will never respond to them.

Jesus teaches us that things can change through prayer. In Matthew 7:7, the Sermon on the Mount, Jesus gives us hope and expectation. "Ask, and it will be given to you; seek, and you will find; knock, and it will be opened to you."

To be able to be an intercessor, you must believe in change. It is essential to understand that God will listen to you and reverse someone's circumstances, attitude, or unbelief.

CHOICE

You have a choice *and* the responsibility to choose correctly.

The sovereign God decided in the beginning to create humans in His own image. Part of that image is that we are not robots. We have the ability and responsibility to choose. Throughout the Word of God, God has honored humans with the ability to choose. The following is an example of this:

> I call heaven and earth to witness against you today, that I have set before you life and death, the blessing and the curse. **So choose life** in order that you may live, you and your descendants. Deuteronomy 30:19.

Joshua chose to follow this advice some forty years later by saying this to the people:

> If it is disagreeable in your sight to serve the LORD, **choose for yourselves today** whom you will serve: whether the gods which your fathers served which were beyond the River, or the gods of the Amorites in whose land you are living; **but as for me and my house, we will serve the LORD**. Joshua 24:15.

In the New Testament, God Himself calls people to make the right choice:

> The Spirit and the bride say, "Come." And let the one who hears say, "Come." And let the one who is thirsty come; **let the one who wishes** take the water of life without cost. Revelation 22:17.

EXAMPLES OF INTERCESSORS CHANGING THINGS

Because we are talking about people being change agents, I have selected a few illustrations from the Old Testament as examples for your encouragement, examples of what can happen when people talk to God.

I have long been impressed by the simplicity of believing prayer. I don't think God ever intended it to be complex.

Elisha was an Old Testament prophet and a man of God. He prayed the simplest of prayers, prayers that any child or brand-new believer could utter.

The first example is in 2 Kings chapter 6 when Elisha and his servant were in a walled city, and this servant got up early in the morning and discovered an enemy's army of horses and chariots had surrounded the city during the night. He was evidently the first one up, as the city alarm had not yet sounded. The purpose of the army was to capture Elisha. The servant was alarmed and asked Elisha what they should do, as their escape was cut off by the surrounding army.

Elisha's first task was to calm the fear of his servant. He said, "Fear not; for they that are with us are more than they that are with them." The servant perceived the might of the enemy; Elisha perceived the overwhelming might of God. To calm his servant, he made this simple petition to God: "O LORD, I pray, open his eyes that he may see." God answered immediately: "And the LORD opened the servant's eyes and he saw; and behold, the mountain was full of horses and chariots of fire all around Elisha." There really was no danger.

Then when the army came down to Elisha, he prayed this second simple prayer: "Elisha prayed to the LORD and said, 'Strike this people with blindness, I pray.' So He struck them with blindness according to the word of Elisha." 2 Kings 6:18.

The prayer is so simple, but the effect is enormous. A whole army was struck blind by a simple prayer of faith. As they were blind, Elisha led them from his town to the capital, Samaria, and into the power of the king. Elisha prayed another simple prayer:

> When they had come into Samaria, Elisha said, "LORD, open the eyes of these *men*, that they may see." So the LORD opened their eyes and they saw; and behold, they were in the midst of Samaria. 2 Kings 6:20.

Could we as intercessors learn to pray after the pattern of Elisha? Prayer would not be so fearsome or complicated, but powerful and world-changing.

The king of Samaria wanted to kill the whole army now in his power, but Elisha saw a greater opportunity. He recommended treating the army kindly, feeding them, and sending them back home as living testimonies to the power of God.

> So he prepared a great feast for them; and when they had eaten and drunk he sent them away, and they went to their master. **And the marauding bands of Arameans did not come again into the land of Israel**. 2 Kings 6:23.

Each soldier had experienced the power of God (blindness) and also the kindness of the God of Israel by the great feast and in being sent back to their families unharmed. This display of the power and kindness of God stopped them from invading anymore.

As we pursue the idea that God has granted humans the ability to be change agents, we see that God responds to us in an amazing way. He often will change what He was going to do according to our prayers or actions.

God is flexible. If we respond to him, He responds to us. God teaches the prophet Ezekiel about His response to us. In chapter 33 He explains that when He says to a wicked person because of his wicked behavior, "You shall surely die," if that person stops being wicked and starts doing right, God will change His mind, and "he shall surely live." That might shock you. He says He has no pleasure in the death of the wicked. His desire is for every person to repent so that God can forgive and restore him or her. What a gracious and forgiving God.

> But when I say to the wicked, "You will surely die," and he turns from his sin and practices justice and righteousness, if a wicked man restores a pledge, pays back what he has taken by robbery, walks by the statutes which ensure life without committing iniquity, he shall surely live; he shall not die. None of his sins that he has committed will be remembered against him. He has practiced justice and righteousness; he shall surely live. Ezekiel 33:14–16.

He has demonstrated that if someone responds to His reproof, He is delighted to change the way He deals with that person.

Sometimes He responds to a request as Jesus promised: "Ask and it will be given you." In the case of King Hezekiah, he had become mortally sick. The Lord sent Isaiah to tell him that he would die of his sickness and should prepare for death. He did not want to die, and he pleaded with the Lord, reminding Him that he had given him wholehearted devotion. God listened to his prayer and decided to add fifteen more years to his life. Think of that. God extended his life span just because he did not want to die at that time. Have you thought that God has a predetermined time for your death and that it cannot be shortened or extended? You need to rethink that assumption.

> In those days Hezekiah became mortally ill. And Isaiah the prophet the son of Amoz came to him and said to him, "Thus says the LORD, 'Set your house in order, for you shall die and not live.'" Then Hezekiah turned his face to the wall and prayed to the LORD, and said, "Remember now, O LORD, I beseech You, how I have walked before You in truth and with a whole heart, and have done what is good in Your sight." And Hezekiah wept bitterly. Then the word of the LORD came to Isaiah, saying, "Go and say to Hezekiah, 'Thus says the LORD, the God of your father David, "I have heard your prayer, I have seen your tears; behold, I will add fifteen years to your life." Isaiah 38:1–5.

Listen to the Word of God: "The fear of the LORD prolongs life, but the years of the wicked will be shortened." Proverbs 10:27.

God is not immune to the voice of humans. In fact, He is very sensitive to our cries. When Joshua was trying to fulfill the task that God had given him to cross over the Jordan River and to conquer the land, he ran into many difficulties. At one time, he had the armies of the Amorites on the run, but daylight was running out, and many of them would escape as a result. So Joshua spoke to the Lord to have the sun stand still until they finished the job. What audacity! What faith! Did the earth stop rotating? What really happened in the sky above? Read about it:

> Then Joshua spoke to the LORD in the day when the LORD delivered up the Amorites before the sons of Israel, and he said in the sight of Israel, "O sun, stand still at Gibeon, And O moon in the valley of Aijalon." So the sun stood still, and the moon stopped, until the nation avenged themselves of their enemies. Is it not written in the book of Jashar? And the sun stopped in the middle of the sky and did not hasten to go *down* for about a whole day. **There was no day like that before it or after it, when the LORD listened to the voice of a man**; for the LORD fought for Israel. Joshua 10:12–14.

Does this prayer of Joshua expand your ideas of what God can and will do? Does this make sense of chapter 2 of this book stating that God can do anything? Let these ideas sink into your heart.

God not only listens to our cries for help in battle, but he also listens to our pleas for his compassion and mercy for others. Moses, who had a close relationship with God, entered into an incredible conversation with God.

> The LORD said to Moses, "I have seen this people, and behold, they are an obstinate people. Now then let Me alone, that My anger may burn against them and that I may destroy them; and I will make of you a great nation."

> "Then Moses entreated the LORD his God, and said, "O LORD, why does Your anger burn against Your people whom You have brought out from the land of Egypt with great power and with a mighty hand? Why should the Egyptians speak, saying, 'With evil *intent* He brought them out to kill them in the mountains and to destroy them from the face of the earth'? Turn from Your burning anger and change Your mind about *doing* harm to Your people. Remember Abraham, Isaac, and Israel, Your servants to whom You swore by Yourself, and said to them, 'I will multiply your descendants as the stars of the heavens, and all this land of which I have spoken I will give to your descendants, and they shall inherit *it* forever.'" So the LORD changed His mind about the harm which He said He would do to His people. Exodus 32:9–14.

Do you recall what I said in the first chapter of this book, that God is looking for intercessors? This incident between God and Moses exemplifies what an intercessor does. Moses, the intercessor, stood between God and the very sinful and rebellious Israelites in the desert. At this point I need to repeat what I said earlier:

> An intercessor is a person of compassion who stands between heaven and earth. With one hand he or she holds the hand of God and with the other holds people, cities, and nations. God, through the ages, has called for intercessors in the fulfillment of His desires.

God found an intercessor in Moses!

Earlier in this chapter was the heading "Choice." I said that God respects our ability to choose and that we should be careful about our choices. As intercessors, we wrestle with many issues, such as understanding our limitations and believing the promises of God to answer "whatever you ask in My name." With this promise, God wants to open wide what we can ask Him to do. But understanding how God responds to humans is essential in the application of these great promises. We have thought together about how God limits His own sovereignty.

When I talk with unbelievers or new believers about these promises, I point out that there are certain unspoken parameters to them. God wants to help them in an unlimited number of issues. But he does not intend to commit unrighteous acts in response to our petitions. I often say, "Don't ask God to help you to rob a bank."

One day the Apostles James and John came up to Jesus with a request:

> James and John, the two sons of Zebedee, came up to Jesus, saying, "Teacher, we want You to do for us whatever we ask of You. And He said to them, "What do you want Me to do for you?" They said to Him, "Grant that we may sit, one on Your right and one on Your left, in Your glory." But Jesus said to them, "You do not know what you are asking...To sit on My right or on My left, this is not Mine to give; but it is for those for whom it has been prepared." Hearing *this*, the ten began to feel indignant with James and John. Mark 10:35–38, 40–41.

In effect, Jesus turned down their request because it was totally self-centered and unjust, so much so that it made the rest of the apostles mad at them.

God can turn down an inappropriate request.

Here is a comparable, amazing concept: *We can turn down what God requests of us!*

> As Jesus went on from there, two blind men followed Him, crying out, "Have mercy on us, Son of David!"
> "When He entered the house, the blind men came up to Him, and Jesus said to them, "Do you believe that I am able to do this?" They said to Him, "Yes, Lord." Then He touched their eyes, saying, "It shall be done to you according to your faith." And their eyes were opened. And Jesus sternly warned them: **"See that no one knows *about this*!"** But they went out and spread the news about Him throughout all that land. Matthew 9:27–31.

Jesus had sternly warned them not to tell anyone about their being healed. They disobeyed what he had commanded them. He had been so merciful and gracious to give them their eyesight that you would think that they would do what he commanded them, but no, they did what they wanted.

Some things about God I find difficult to understand, especially when He desires to do good for men and they don't want Him to. Why doesn't He just overrule them and do good to them anyway?

One day Jesus told His disciples to get into a boat and head for the east side of the Sea of Galilee where the Gadarenes lived. It was Gentile country that had at one time belonged to Israel. There he cast out many demons from two demonized men. They lived in the tombs and were so violent that they would not allow anyone to travel the road near them.

The demons that he cast out entered a large herd of swine that belonged to the nearby city. The demons gave the swine the impulse to rush headlong down the hillside, and they drowned in the lake. It was a herd of about two thousand pigs. This represented a great loss to the city.

> And behold, the whole city came out to meet Jesus; and when they saw Him, **they implored Him to leave their region**. Getting into a boat, Jesus crossed over the sea and came to His own city. Matthew 8:34; 9:1.

He could have stayed there and have healed every sick person as He had done in many other cities, but He went away because they had begged Him to go. What do we learn about God and about prayer from this incident?

I think it is possible for a person to reject God even though God desires to enter his or her life. God does not force Himself onto people, though He does actively work on drawing them to Himself.

The Apostle Paul in his ministry confronted unbelievers with the good news of salvation by faith in Jesus, the Lamb of God. When the Jews opposed his message, he left them for the gentiles, who were also unbelieving but had not taken a stand against Christ. He made every effort to reach all of them, both Jews and Gentiles. He worked on persuading them. He declares in 2 Corinthians 5:11, "Knowing the fear of the Lord, we persuade men."

I don't think the rejection of Jesus by the Gadarenes was considered by Jesus as permanent. The Gospel of Mark adds this comment about the same incident:

> As He was getting into the boat, the man who had been demon-possessed was imploring Him that he might accompany Him. And He did not let him, but He said to him, "Go home to your people and report to them what great things the Lord has done for you, and how He had mercy on you." And he went away and began to proclaim in Decapolis what great things Jesus had done for him; and everyone was amazed. Mark 5:18–20.

Jesus left, but he did not give up on them. He sent a messenger to continue to live among them to draw them to Christ, one of their own who had experienced the grace of Christ.

This week I received an e-mail from a believer who lives in Norwich, England, who commented, "You mentioned godless people. Norwich, which is a fine city and which is a lovely place to live, is known as the most godless city in the United Kingdom as so few people in a survey acknowledge any religious affiliation."

This man and his wife are wonderful living examples of the grace of Christ. They are privileged to be living, bright lights in a dark environment, just as the Gadarene was.

As I pray for people who do not believe the Gospel, I often ask myself as I pray for them, "What would it take for them to be persuaded?" Sometimes it is the love of Christ that is the persuader, and for others it is the realization that they may be missing heaven or even the fear of hell. One person I am praying for is dead to the concept of God. I am praying for the Holy Spirit to make that person's spirit alive to God and aware of His existence.

Seven or eight years ago, I heard of a US congressman who was not a believer but whose wife was. In desperation one day, she gathered some other wives to pray for him while he was in Washington. Later he recounted to his wife that as he was sitting in session, he had the eerie sense that God was watching him. This happened day after day until he acknowledged Christ and came to him. He had become aware of their prayer meetings and asked his wife when they started praying. He concluded that the same day they had begun praying is when he had the sense that God was watching him. God has many ways of creating a desire in people to want to find him.

You can see from these illustrations of answered prayer that God has done many things that the world would not believe that He will do. Many of us believers have a hard time believing it too. As intercessors, we need to ask God to give us a believing heart for the written Word of God. As we have read, God has in response to prayer revealed angelic chariots of fire around us and halted the course of the sun and of the moon; He has even made them to go backward. Jesus told the wind and the waves, "Peace, be still," and a great calm came immediately. Just the miracles of Jesus would fill page after page if we were to stop and enumerate them. Read the Gospels over and over again, and let their extensiveness fill your mind and heart.

Jesus took three years to let the disciples witness His power day after day. Sometimes Jesus even granted to them, in His name, to also do these miracles (read Luke chapters 9 and 10). They learned the proper use of the name of Jesus, to glorify God in the way they used this name. They learned that they should not be seeking their own will or their own desires but rather those of their Father in Heaven.

With these three years of training in God's ways behind them, on the last night of Jesus's time with them, He opened the limitless windows of heaven to them by giving to them astounding promises. Even more astounding, it seems that these same promises are available to all of His children if they meet the conditions. In these promises, asking becomes a world-changing event.

> Whatever you ask in My name, that will I do, so that the Father may be glorified in the Son. If you ask Me anything in My name, I will do it. John 14:13–14.

I searched the Greek and many translations of the Bible, and it turns out that the above means exactly what it says, with a few insignificant grammatical changes. What you read is what Jesus meant. Two phrases supporting the same idea in this portion catch my attention: "Whatever you ask in My name…If you ask Me anything in My name, I will do it."

In saying "whatever" and "anything," Jesus is giving them some of the most powerful tools in the universe. They stagger the human imagination. Now do you see why in chapter 1 I said, "You can be God's instrument to change people, cities, and nations"?

These promises are the culmination of God's ways of including godly men and women in bringing His power to bear upon earth and heaven. He fully intended for us to use these promises to glorify Him on the earth. He wants the following to be our motive, "so that the Father may be glorified in the Son."

Do you see more clearly now why he preceded this promise with, "Truly, truly, I say to you, he who believes in Me, the works that I do, he will do also; and greater works than these he will do; because I go to the Father"? John 14:12.

I have a computer program that requires an activation code to release all of its very powerful features. It seems that this promise of, "If you ask Me anything in My name, I will do it," requires an activation code word as stated in the following verse: "And all things you ask in prayer, **believing**, you will receive." Matthew 21:22.

What we have read in this chapter leads us to believe that the promises by Jesus for prayer are meant to open huge doors for us. God calls us to very large opportunities to glorify Him and to advance His Kingdom. The question remains if we will activate our faith to see these promises fulfilled.

As a young person, I heard a sermon by a man of God named Don Hillis. He was a missionary statesman, as was his brother, Dick Hillis. Don made a statement that so impressed me that I wrote it in my Bible to never forget it. He said, "You only really believe that which activates you!" It is simple but profound.

It is similar to the statement that we find in the book of James: "Faith without works is dead." If we say we believe these promises but do not act on them, Don Hillis says that we don't really believe them. We always are in danger of falling into the category of the hearers of the words of the prophet Ezekiel. God said of Ezekiel,

> Behold, you are to them like a sensual song by one who has a beautiful voice and plays well on an instrument; for they hear your words but they do not practice them. Ezekiel 33:32.

As you think about these promises from God, do you have the sense that God is looking down upon you and saying, "Well, what will you do with these priceless promises?"

We have three choices like the following people had.

1. Matthew 19:21, 22: "Jesus said, 'Sell your possessions…come follow me'…he went away sorrowful." We can decide not to in unbelief.
2. Luke 9:59: "Permit me to first go and bury my father." Delayed opportunity. Wait awhile, Jesus, he is saying.
3. Matthew 4:19, 20: Follow me…immediately they left their nets and followed him. Yes, now is the time. This is the faith that leads to action.

What is the decision? The question is, "Will I become an intercessor, claiming these promises by faith?" Make a decision now and become one of the change agents for Christ. God will honor your decision and will be working with you. E-mail me at jackblanch@mindspring.com. I will send you prayer-encouragement e-mails every now and then. Welcome to the growing number of committed intercessors.

> *Dear Father, understanding Your personality is such an intimate thing. We need to know what to do with any understanding that You grant to us about Yourself. May I treat any light that You give to me as a man would treat an intimate heart revelation from his lover about herself. May it be*

personal and precious to me. I perceive that You treat Your children born by Your Spirit with infinite more intimacy than those outside of Your family. I understand that Your love is an abiding love over all, but Your intimacy is reserved for Your family. May any insight that You give us about how You relate to others be precious in our sight.

4

God Listens to Children

How old do you have to be to no longer be a child? Could this chapter be for you no matter what age you are? Most people who pick up this book on prayer and about being a change agent in the world will be adults. Can I speak to you as a child? I hope this will not offend you.

Child, your Father in Heaven is listening carefully. Every plea of yours reaches Him. Every groan, every doubt, every confused thought ascends upward and reaches all the way to the throne of the Majesty on High. Does a child need to have a broken arm for his or her father or mother to immediately respond to it? Can it be a small scrape on the elbow, a stubbed toe, a little girl's cry of frustration that a curl will not stay in place? The difficulty does not need to be big; it only needs to be big to the child, a matter to cry about.

As a child grows older and cries about something, a father often says, "Stop being a child, and take it like a man." So as we mature, we learn to not cry, to cover up our pain, and to act like adults. Too bad for humanity, the cover-up continues for years.

If you have been born of God, there is a special relationship between you and the Father. If you don't think you have this relationship, it can easily be established. The Apostle John, the one who was leaning on Jesus's lap at the Last Supper, said in the introduction of his Gospel, "To all who did receive Him, He gave them the right to be children of God, to those who believe in

His name." John 1:12 (HCSB). Just believing in Jesus and receiving him gives us the right to call ourselves a child of God. How simple and yet so profound. If you apply what you are reading, this book will be a great profit for you. If you believe that Jesus is the Son of God but have never invited Him to enter your life and to run it, bow your head right now and humbly ask Him to enter you and to be your ruler. This is the beginning of praying by faith. You can, from this moment on, talk to God as His child because you have believed in Jesus and have received Him. You have extended an invitation to him to enter your life and to transform you. You have become His child, and all that I am writing applies to you.

The above paragraph assumes that you know quite a bit about Jesus. But if you know almost nothing about Him, then you need to learn something about Him before inviting Him into your life. There are two commonly used passages about Jesus and receiving Him. I have already mentioned John 1:12: "But as many as received Him, to them He gave the right to become children of God, even to those who believe in His name."

Who is this Jesus? John says that Jesus is the Word of God and that this Word was actually God. He is the Son of God. A few paragraphs further on in John chapter 1, one of His new followers declares, "Rabbi, You are the Son of God; You are the King of Israel." So when you receive Jesus, you must be aware of this, because when He comes into your life, He comes in to be your king and ruler. I had to face that the evening I invited Jesus into my life.

I saw my need to become a child of God by accepting Him and was reading what Jesus said: **"Behold, I stand at the door and knock; if anyone hears My voice and opens the door, I will come in to him and will dine with him, and he with Me."** Revelation 3:20. I believed He was the Son of God, but at that moment I also had to come face to face with the fact that He was the king, the ruler of heaven and earth. Realizing this, I understood that He would come into my life to rule it. This idea produced a moment of fear as I wondered what He would do with my life if He ruled it. I pictured myself driving a car and suddenly inviting Jesus into the car to take the steering wheel. Would He drive me over a cliff and destroy me? I had been reading about His life in the Gospels and had seen how caring and gentle He was with people. I thought, *No, He will drive me into better paths than I am taking myself. I can trust Him.* My fear left me, and I told Him that I would follow Him and that He could guide my life when He came in.

HUMILITY

The foremost characteristic of children, as Jesus pointed out, is humility. Let's listen to what He says to His disciples.

> And He called a child to Himself and set him before them, and said, "Truly I say to you, unless you are converted and become like children, you will not enter the kingdom of heaven. Whoever then humbles himself as this child, he is the greatest in the kingdom of heaven." Matthew 18:2–4.

King David of Israel took this childlike position in one of the Psalms; he wrote:

> O LORD, my heart is not proud, nor my eyes haughty; Nor do I involve myself in great matters, or in things too difficult for me. Surely I have composed and quieted my soul; like a weaned child rests against his mother. My soul is like a weaned child within me. Psalm 131:1–2.

Can you imagine a king publicly saying, "Nor do I involve myself in great matters or in things too difficult for me"? Let's try to join David in this humble position.

When my children were small, they loved it when I sat on the floor with them, when I got down to their level. Can you picture the Heavenly Father sitting on the floor with you? Could you imagine just sitting with Him, the two of you on the floor?

One day God gave to King David a promise that his descendent would reign forever [the Christ]. David was so humbled that "David the king went in **and sat before the LORD** and said, 'Who am I, O LORD God, and what is my house that You have brought me this far?'"1 Chronicles 17:16.

Can we, as intercessors, become children? A child starts communicating with his or her father or mother with the simplest communication—a cry, a whimper, a smile. Later, communication turns to conversation: "I want…I need…Gimme." These phases are totally acceptable to a parent. Every parent soon teaches his or her child to say, "Thank you." As we express our needs and wants to our Father, we are learning how to pray.

In the Sermon on the Mount, Jesus teaches His "children" many things about prayer. He not only teaches us how to pray and how not to pray; He also teaches how the Father cares for us:

> Look at the birds of the air, that they do not sow, nor reap nor gather into barns, and yet your heavenly Father feeds them. Are you not worth much more than they? Matthew 6:26.

It will be very difficult for us to pray for others with confidence and faith until we are convinced that our Father cares for us. So it is important to start by praying for yourself, to learn to have a one-on-one conversation with God. I have a prayer list to help me to remember to pray for the most important things. The first item on my list is this:

> Talk with my Father. Jesus said, "I am the true vine, and My Father is the vinedresser." John 15:1.

> I, the LORD, am its keeper; I water it every moment. So that no one will damage it, I guard it night and day. Isaiah 27:3.

This is actually what I have written. I want to remind myself that my Father, my Dad, hovers over me to protect me. I love Him for this. He is deeply interested in every facet of my life. We enjoy each other.

As you draw near to your Heavenly Father, the Holy Spirit teaches you about Him. He wants to give you good things. If you ask Him to do something that you don't realize is bad for you, you will soon realize He ignores your request or gives you something better.

Jesus taught us in the Sermon on the Mount the following:

> If you then, being evil, know how to give good gifts to your children, how much more will your Father who is in heaven give what is good to those who ask Him! Matthew 7:11.

A recent believer, upon learning that I am writing a book on prayer, asked me to tell you that from his new experience with Christ, He will often answer us differently than what we have asked for.

In our spiritual immaturity, we often ask wrongly. But as Jesus said, our Father in Heaven will figure out what is good for us and give us that.

This is my personal prayer: *"Jesus, thank You for including me in Your family. I don't deserve it, but I love it. I am old and forget a lot of things. But I still need Your help very often throughout the day. Help me to remember what I need to remember. Thank You."*

The following is a summary verse from the Old Testament prophet Micah.

> He has told you, O man, what is good; and what does the LORD require of you but to do justice, to love kindness, and to walk humbly with your God? Micah 6:8.

Your Heavenly Father Desires a Relationship with You

A child often thinks of his or her parents as givers, but that is not the only way the child thinks of them. When I would come home from work, my children would run to the door to be able to jump into my arms as I entered. They love their parents and cling to them. The parents love it when a child does this. How it warms our hearts. Figure out for yourself how to figuratively jump into your Heavenly Father's arms. Do it often. He is not just a giver; he is a loving father.

Why do you think that Jesus said that the *most important* commandment of the Old Testament is to love the Lord our God with all of our heart, soul, and mind? Fathers and mothers desire above all else to be loved by their children.

As I visited my five-year-old grandson this week, the first thing that he asked me was to play a game with him. Was he really interested in the game or in relating? Children don't say, "Let's relate," do they? They say it by looking for something to do together.

When God created Adam and Eve, the Bible records that God created a garden. We call a group of fruit trees an orchard. God created an orchard of beautiful fruit trees through which He and Adam and Eve could stroll. Why? Because God wanted to relate with them. Prayer can be seen as having a good chat or a stroll with our Father.

There is an old hymn that goes like this:

"My God and I go into the fields together, we walk and talk just as good friends should and do. We clasp our hands, our voices ring with laughter. My God and I shall go unendingly."

For me, this is not just a song—it is an emotional memory. As a new believer, I often visited a relative's ranch when I lived in the city. I would walk through a wheat field, singing this song and enjoying fellowship with my newfound Jesus. Do you have someplace where you and God enjoy meeting? Go there as often as you can.

When we lived in Spain, there was a beautiful cathedral just a short walk from our house. My wife would go there to commune with God. It was quiet, private, beautiful, and worshipful.

My prayer: *"God, I am so privileged to be called Your son. I feel like I can just walk into Your throne room as if I belong there—well, actually, I do. I am Your eternal son, not because I merit it, but because You fathered me."*

Honesty and Sincerity

To pray like a child, we may need to learn all over again to pray. By that I mean that children's conversations with their parents are normally honest and open. They say what they are thinking, not what adults think is right to say.

How often have you been embarrassed in public by a comment that burst forth from your child?

Have you learned to pray as others think you ought to pray? You may need to cast aside this way of praying so that you can pray as a child. Praying as an adult often means praying as a hypocrite. How often have you prayed the Lord's Prayer without meaning a bit of it, praying in total insincerity? "Thy will be done," you say in prayer, but do you really mean "My will be done"?

Yesterday I was in the barbershop awaiting my turn for a haircut. A mother was there with two children about two and three years old. She was trying to keep them entertained while their dad was getting his hair cut. They had some crayons and a coloring book. When it was time to go, she gathered up the coloring books and started to put away the crayons. The two-year-old tightly grasped the crayons and ran toward the door to get away from his mom. "Not her will, but my will be done," was his idea. Have you been in the habit of praying, "Thy will be done" and then closing your fist tightly, holding on to your own will?

In the portion of the Lord's Prayer, "Forgive us our debts as we forgive our debtors," do you really want God to forgive you the way you forgive others? But you pray that often, don't you, if you repeat the Lord's Prayer? Set aside your hypocrisy and pray what you really mean. Well, maybe not, because what your heart really wants may be a bad thing. Has your prayer been an ugly thing to God, a totally insincere prayer? Can you confess to God that you have been praying as a hypocrite and ask Him to help you to pray an honest, open prayer filled with good requests? Would He answer that type of prayer?

To begin to learn to pray with sincerity, you may even need to stop praying memorized prayers for a while, like "Our Father," until you can pray all of it sincerely. One good way to enter into God's presence with sincerity may be to practice what I practice when in church. As we sing a hymn, I stop singing when we get to a portion that would be hypocritical for me to sing. Try it. You may find that you can sincerely only sing about half of a particular hymn. This will bring sincerity to your life and to your relationship with God. Take heart. God loves to answer His children when they ask sincerely for a good thing.

As you consider these illustrations, don't become reluctant to pray. We don't need to pray perfect prayers any more than children feel that they must be careful how they word things as they talk to their parents. God is an understanding Father. He does want honesty but not perfection in how we phrase our communication with Him.

Jesus, shortly after He gives us the sample prayer of "Our Father," encourages us to pray by saying, "Ask, and it will be given to you." Please note that He does not fill this sentence with qualifiers such as, "ask, being careful that you ask the right things" or "ask in the right tone" or "don't ask for too much."

Children learn what to ask by asking. The parent will respond, and the child will learn from the parent's response what is appropriate to ask.

The main idea of Jesus's sermon is to encourage the disciples to ask, expecting answers. God has no limit to what He can do, and there is no end to what He can supply. He never responds with a comment that He just ran out of this or that. He is a creator. He can make anything out of nothing.

Jesus attended a wedding feast very early on in His ministry. He was accompanied by five new disciples who had been with Him just a couple of days. His whole family was invited, so Mary was there, too. An embarrassing situation came up; they ran out of wine for the wedding guests. Mary approached Jesus with the problem, saying, "They have no wine." Jesus responded, "Woman, what does this have to do with us?" She could have turned and walked away at this rather brusque answer, but she did not.

Sometimes the original Aramaic language doesn't translate easily into English. When Jesus said, "Ask and it will be given you," the Aramaic verb for "ask" is better translated, "Ask and keep on asking, seek and keep on seeking, knock and keep on knocking." In other words, don't give up easily.

Mary exemplifies this truth when they ran out of wine by turning to the servants and saying, "Whatever he says to you, do it." The result was that Jesus, being a creator, changed about 150 gallons of water into wine. Mary asked, expecting an answer, and Jesus wants us to ask that way also.

A child's way of asking is without considering any ramifications of his or her request. He or she doesn't think about how much it costs. Children just say, for example, "I want a pony." Maybe they live in an apartment and don't have a yard. That happened to us. Our son, Danny, wanted a rhinoceros. Children just ask and keep on asking without consideration of the details. Jesus says to ask that way. Don't try to work out the details. Ask persistently, but don't try to tell God how to do His job.

Writing about a child praying is difficult for me. I can only use others' children or my own children as examples, because, growing up, my parents took me to church but never, that I can recall, taught me to pray. Please, teach your children to pray. As they receive answers, they will become convinced of the reality of God.

My prayer: *"Forgive me for singing things I did not mean. I have some trouble being sincere with people because I want to say nice things to them even if they are not true. I like people to like me. What can you do for me? Amen."*

A Childlike Faith

A child can pray a great prayer. There is simplicity to childlike faith. It is a pure faith without understanding. What do I mean by this?

Pure faith to me means that it is not mixed with doubt. A child has the capacity to just simply believe his or her parents or others. The word is "ingenuous." It means free from reserve, sincere, innocent, and naive.

Without understanding means to me that the child does not comprehend the processes or depth behind an issue. The child is free of the mental processes that complicate our adult lives and make it difficult for us to believe. The following is an illustration of this type of faith quoted from my book *Disciple Making for a New Generation*, chapter 6, "Growing in Faith," page 68:

> One hot summer day in Madrid, our old refrigerator stopped running. It was so old that you could clearly hear if it were running or not. I had repeatedly repaired it and now thought that it was in its final gasp. The end had come.
>
> A couple of hours later the family sat down to have lunch. Before thanking God for our food, our son, Danny, who was six said, "Dad,

> pray for God to fix our refrigerator!" Gulp! There were two other little sets of eyes looking at me, our three-year-old daughter and our one-year-old daughter, plus my wife's eyes. I knew too much about our refrigerator to believe that a little prayer would resurrect it. I had no faith that God would respond to my prayer for it. However, it was obvious that my son believed that God could do this. Not wanting to be a hypocrite and pray for something that I did not believe would come to pass, I said, "Danny, why don't you pray for it as you thank the Lord for the meal?"
>
> I can hear you thinking right now: *What a cop-out.* I am afraid you are right. Well, anyway, Danny prayed, asking God to fix the refrigerator, and gave thanks for the meal. We were about two minutes into our meal when we heard a noise from the kitchen. Yes, you guessed it—the refrigerator had started up of its own accord! I was surprised, but not Danny; he just kept on eating his meal. The entire time that we rented that apartment, the refrigerator never had another problem.

Are you a new believer and feel like a novice in prayer? Or are you an older believer beginning to see God as your loving Father who wants to take care of you? Can you sincerely say to your Father, "I don't know what to do; guide me and help me"?

He loves to answer prayers like this. James, the leader of the church in Jerusalem, wrote a book of the New Testament simply titled "James." He wrote a number of one-liners that are profound and simple. He said, "Draw near to God and He will draw near to you." James 4:8. The sample prayer above is sufficient for God to respond to you and to actually draw near to you. Just pray it with confidence that He hears you.

Maybe you have been a believer for years but have not seen God helping you, and so you have become an unbeliever about prayer. A very common experience for me is to encounter Christians who have ceased to believe that God will help them. Some years ago, they probably ceased to hope in God and, as a result, make their own way in life without His help. Theirs is a Christian life without God.

Do you think it is possible to start anew after so many years? Can your faith be resurrected? It will start with humbling yourself before God and getting on your knees right now with a simple prayer such as, *"My Father, can we start over again? Even though I regularly attend church, my soul has been wandering in a parched desert for years, a desert of unbelief. My family and I are dying out here in the desert. Please rescue us."*

Or maybe, in sincerity, the following prayer may be more like your present state of feelings: *"Father, I am really mad at You. I feel like You have not paid attention to me. You have let bad things happen to me that no father should allow. Would you help me to get over how I feel about You? Help me, God!"*

Is there hope for you if you pray this simple prayer in sincerity? Will God ignore you and say it is too late? Or is He like the father of the Prodigal Son who has been waiting years with arms open, desiring to hear a prayer like this? There is hope for you who have been angry with God and have been rebellious as a result.

In your desert experience, Christ, the Living Water, has been right there but unseen by you. He has been unseen partially because He has not done what you wanted the way you wanted it. This blinds you to the presence of Christ. As you humble yourself before Him, He reveals His presence. There is a well of water in the desert.

As an encouragement for those of you who have been having a desert-soul experience, God offers the following story in Genesis chapter 21. See if you can picture yourself in these events.

Sarah, the wife of Abraham, has a handmaiden called Hagar who, at Sarah's request, has a son called Ishmael by Abraham. When Sarah finally has a son, Isaac, thirteen years later, problems arise, and Hagar and her son are banished to the desert.

> So, Abraham rose early in the morning and took bread and a skin of water and gave them to Hagar, putting them on her shoulder, and gave her the boy, and sent her away. And she departed and **wandered about in the wilderness of Beersheba**.

> ¹⁵When the water in the skin was used up, she left the boy under one of the bushes.
> ¹⁶Then she went and sat down opposite him, about a bowshot away, for she said, "Do not let me see the boy die." And she sat opposite him, and lifted up her voice and wept.
> ¹⁷**God heard the lad crying**; and the angel of God called to Hagar from heaven and said to her, "What is the matter with you, Hagar? Do not fear, for God has heard the voice of the lad where he is. Arise, lift up the lad, and hold him by the hand, for I will make a great nation of him." **Then God opened her eyes and she saw a well of water; and she went and filled the skin with water and gave the lad a drink.** Genesis 21:14–19.

God was aware of them all the time and had a well of water that she could not see. God has never abandoned you. You just have become blind to His presence and the water available to you. Jesus has always said, "Come unto me, you who are weary and faint, and I will give you rest." He has compassion for the weary and confused.

Go back to the beginning of this chapter and review it. Ask yourself what God had spoken to you about. In the margin or in the following blank space in this book, jot a note to God, responding to what you feel He had said to you. God would love to hear from you, His child.

Dear Father,

____

____

____

____

____

5

Believing the Promises of God

When it comes to prayer, God has made many great promises. The challenge is to believe them and to put them into the use that God purposed for them. The Apostle Peter describes them this way:

> For by these He has granted to us **His precious and magnificent promises**, so that by them you may become partakers of the divine nature, having escaped the corruption that is in the world by lust. 2 Peter 1:4.

His precious and magnificent promises enable us to share in the Divine Nature as we believe them and possess them as our own. It is impossible to overstate their importance for Christ-like living. These promises also become the basis for prayers of faith; however, these prayers of faith must be subject to the will of God. He is preeminent.

> This is the confidence which we have before Him, that, **if we ask anything according to His will, He hears us**. And if we know that He hears us in whatever we ask, we know that we have the requests which we have asked from Him. 1 John 5:14–15.

Jesus exemplified the importance of prayer and living by God's will as He summarized this in His purpose statement:

> But so that the world may know that I love the Father, I do exactly as the Father commanded Me. Get up, let us go from here. John 14:31.

Confidence in prayer comes through knowing that we have prayed according to His will. There are many promises about prayer, but the unspoken condition is as Jesus prayed in Gethsemane.

> And He went a little beyond them, and fell on His face and prayed, saying, "My Father, if it is possible, let this cup pass from Me; yet not as I will, but as You will." Matthew 26:39.

Praying in the will of God is a sign of our love for God. On the last night before dying, He left the eleven Apostles a number of promises in John chapters 14, 15, and 16. Only one promise would have been sufficient, but it would seem that He was trying to make a lasting impression on them through repetition.

> **Whatever you ask** in My name, that will I do, so that the Father may be glorified in the Son. If you **ask Me anything** in My name, I will do it. John 14:13–14.

> If you abide in Me, and My words abide in you, **ask whatever you wish**, and it will be done for you. John 15:7.

> You did not choose Me but I chose you, and appointed you that you would go and bear fruit, and that your fruit would remain, so that **whatever you ask** of the Father in My name He may give to you. John 15:16.

> In that day you will not question Me about anything. Truly, truly, I say to you, if you **ask the Father for anything** in My name, He will

give it to you. Until now you have asked for nothing in My name; ask and you will receive, so that your joy may be made full. John 16:23–24.

Notice the repeated wording:

- **"Whatever you ask"—John 14:13.**
- **"Ask Me anything"—John 14:14.**
- **"Ask whatever you wish"—John 15:7.**
- **"Whatever you ask"—John 15:16.**
- **"Ask the Father for anything"—John 16:23.**

What is Jesus trying to get across to them? Limitless asking, asking according to what they see as important.

As I look over this list, "Ask whatever you wish" draws my attention. This was originally written in Greek, and the idea is "anything you desire." What are my desires? I desire that four people who I know would become wholehearted followers of Jesus. They don't know Him at all. I believe that reading about Jesus in the Gospel of John would be the way forward for them.

One of these four is D——. His mother was born in Spain, and Spanish is his first language, although he is fluent in English and is going to college in Colorado Springs. I, too, am fluent in Spanish. This morning I downloaded the Bible in Spanish to my tablet to have it available for him.

Encouraged by this promise, I just wrote down three desires of my heart; two of them are in the preceding paragraph. I am living in a senior residence, it is 4:00 a.m., and D—— works the night shift. I just stepped into the elevator and got off at the second floor. As I exited, D—— was walking by! I showed him the downloaded Spanish Bible, and it really pleased him. I asked him if he had ever read the words of Jesus. He said only as a child. I encouraged him to read it as an adult.

I offered to read it with him for about fifteen or twenty minutes. He said tomorrow morning about 3:30 a.m. would work for him. We have an appointment.

I am writing about prayer, but I must confess that even I am amazed that my prayer for D—— on the basis of John 15:7 was answered in less than fifteen minutes! These promises are real! I am so happy about the prospect of tomorrow morning. It brings John 16:24 to mind: "Ask and you will receive, so **that your joy may be made full**."

Jesus links faith to the use of these amazing promises. A few days prior to giving them these promises, He taught them about faith and the promises.

As He was entering Jerusalem one morning during that eventful week, He was hungry and approached a fig tree that was found to be fruitless. Jesus pronounced death to the tree, and the next day they observed it dying or dead. When the apostles commented with amazement on how rapidly the tree had died, Jesus said:

> Truly I say to you, if you have faith and do not doubt, you will not only do what was done to the fig tree, but even if you say to this mountain, "Be taken up and cast into the sea," it will happen. **And all things you ask in prayer, believing, you will receive**. Matthew 21:21–22.

Do you read this promise and think, "That is really interesting," and your thoughts go no further? Or, on the contrary, possibly you are one of those persons who thinks, "Wow, I can ask anything that I believe God wants to do and expect Him to do it. Through faith, even I can become a world changer." You don't have to ponder it for a month or a year to believe this. The promises are right there for the picking, so to speak. You can just reach up and grab one and make it yours for the glory of God.

Delay signifies doubt and a lack of trusting what your Savior offers to you. General promises like these (open to all) are just waiting to be possessed by any of us. How deeply disturbing it must be to Christ to see so many of us observe them and then pass on our way without harvesting even one of them. It is like we are saying, "These are interesting for someone, but they are not for me."

How long have you been reading the Bible? How many times have you personally passed right on over these "**precious and magnificent promises**" that Peter wrote about? Have you been reading the Bible for five years, ten years, forty years? Will you keep passing by those words?

I had been a believer for about one or two years (a churchgoer since childhood), when I heard a man named Dawson Trotman give a message on believing these promises. He pointed out that they were for anyone who believed them. He then challenged us to believe that God would use any of us to claim a nation or a continent for Christ.

You could see that he meant it because he was reaching out to the nations himself. He was being used to prepare and send men and women to the world. As he spoke I could see that he really believed that any of us listening could be that person.

God stirred up a spirit of faith in me that I had never known before. I believed for the first time in my life that God could use *me* to reach out to a nation that needed Christ. From that day on, I took to heart the promise of "**Ask for anything in my name**" and asked Him to send me to a nation that needed Christ. I grabbed hold of that promise that Jesus had made.

I believe that no matter what your past or present, no matter your health or hindrances, you can, with God's help, be a person to claim these promises and make a difference in the world. As I write this, I am greatly encouraged and know that some of you will believe these promises and become world changers in your part of the world or in another part. Praise be to God!

I said I asked God to use me to touch a needy nation. Eighteen years later my wife and I found ourselves in Spain, calling the nation to Christ. He sent us to a region that historically had almost no people of faith in Jesus. People had been baptized as children into Catholicism, but as they grew older, they had rejected the idea of God. College and high-school students, for the most part, were Catholic atheists. We brought faith to a region that had only known good works but nothing about faith in Jesus. What an enormous privilege. As these students would come to know Christ, they would comment that they knew of no other believer in Jesus as the Way in their town. None of their parents, grandparents, or great-grandparents had ever believed in Jesus, they said. They were deeply touched that they were the first and often wondered why.

Think about the world. Are there any places left on the earth where people have not believed in Jesus? Is there a town or village that has only worshiped idols for centuries, or that has worshiped no one (atheist) or Vishnu, Shiva, Buddha, their ancestors, Mother Earth, or some other god? Would you consider it a privilege to be the first to proclaim Jesus, the Son of God, there? Maybe in your own family line you have been the first to trust in Christ that you know of. My wife was the first in her immediate family, although her grandmother had been a believer. She was used by God to influence her entire immediate family to know Christ.

There is still plenty of room in the world and in our nation for people who will yet ask God to use them in this capacity. Can you expect to be used by God among disabled people, cancer patients, or others? There is plenty to believe God for. The world is still needy.

Maybe we can get past ourselves and get a vision for others. Just a few days after Jesus gave the apostles these promises, he rose from the dead and commanded them to go to Galilee where he would meet them. There he gave them the command to go into all the world. *They would need these promises to do this.* The promises are meant to be used to fulfill God's purposes. What are God's purposes for you?

God has placed each of us into a special world of influence, relatives, friends, work place, and so on. These promises were not given exclusively for evangelism but also for our benefit and for the others in your world of influence. Open your eyes. Is there no place where these promises could be useful?

Usually believing is a process of growth. Jesus spoke of no faith, little faith, and great faith.

What is a prayer of faith? The simplest definition that I know of is that you believe that God will give you what you ask for. It is a prayer of rest because if you believe that God will give you what you have asked, you rest in peace, knowing that the answer will come in God's time.

> This is the confidence which we have before Him, that, if we ask anything according to His will, He hears us. And if we know that He

hears us in whatever we ask, we know that we have the requests which we have asked from Him. 1 John 5:14–15.

This was written by the Apostle John, who was present that last night when Jesus made that wonderful group of promises. He expresses that a prayer of faith leads to a sure confidence that what we have asked for is ours already. After asking with faith, the most natural result of this is confidence, is a prayer of praise with joy that the answer is coming. A prayer of doubt results in hoping that something will happen; that kind of prayer does not result in joy, because you have no confidence that the answer is on the way.

What should we do if, after praying for something, we doubt that the answer will come? For me this is a common situation. I sometimes pray hoping.

I suppose everyone has a different approach to doubt. I do two things if I doubt that I will receive what I am asking:

1. I review what I know about God. I ask myself if He would like to answer this.
2. I review prayer promises that I know. Is there some promise of God that deals with this issue?

My wife has a bad knee that bothers her a lot. "God, will you take away the pain? I hope so." Is it the will of God to take away her pain? One of our goals in life is this: "That I may know Him and the power of His resurrection and **the fellowship of His sufferings**, being conformed to His death." Philippians 3:10.

Part of this goal is "fellowship of His suffering." Is this knee problem part of this? We know you can heal and want to, if the occasion is right. We trust you to do the right thing. A month ago you were pleased to take away her chronic back pain. Your mercies rest upon us.

Through the Apostle Paul in the letter to the Galatians, the Lord teaches us about how faith works.

Faith works by love: "For in Christ Jesus neither circumcision nor uncircumcision means anything, but faith working through love." Galatians 5:6.

"Faith working through love" is a marvelous revelation from God. We have been given these great promises for prayer that love can be activated through believing. If I don't love people very much, I am not activated to believe on their behalf. Their situation does not move me to claim a promise for them. How often have I seen a relative's or friend's need and thought that *they* need to take some action? That may be true, but it is also true that I could take some action in believing prayer. Disinterest in helping them leaves the promises unused.

A number of these promises are listed on the first page of this chapter. What if you made a list of the people around you and their needs and then matched one of the promises with each person? Love requires an investment of time. To make this list would require time. Could life become really meaningful for you in a new way? Would joy enter your heart as you think of the changes that could come about for them?

Let me give you a couple of tips:

- Jesus recommended for us to sometimes "go into your closet and pray in secret." Keep this prayer list between you and God.
- What people think they need is often not what they need. Effective prayer depends on guidance from the Holy Spirit. Come before God and ask Him if the need that you listed after each person is what God would put as the primary need for him or her. He will guide you to cross off some things and modify the need.
- Watch expectantly for the answers. Put the date you started praying for these items on the list, and you will see God's timetable.

Now think about your church, city, nation, or the world and their needs. Ask God for one thing that you should be praying about for one of these categories. Ask for just one, please. Don't get overloaded in prayer at this time. Start simply.

God says faith works by love. Loving people should result in praying the promises for them. We have been given the resources to help them by faith. But loving people is not the only thing. How about loving God? What is on the Father's heart, and what is on Jesus's heart? You are on Their hearts, and the world is on Their hearts. Could one of the purposes of these promises be to fulfill God's desires? You may be thinking that God does what He wants and fulfills His own desires. What does this have to do with me?

He uses humans to extend the message of salvation, to call people, to woo people to Him. Have you not seen that yet? God commissions *us* to call people to Him. He fills us with love to draw people. "I drew them with cords of a man, with bands of love." Hosea 11:4. (KJV).

What is the importance of love? God's love draws people, and God's love through us draws people. In the above, He talks about ropes and bonds. Love is the "tie that binds." It is not only the tie that binds us to Him or that draws us to Him. Love is also what thrusts us out to other people. Second Corinthians 5:14 (NIV) says that the love of Christ *compels* us—that is, thrusts us out to reach the people who are on God's heart. "Now all these things are from God, who reconciled us to Himself through Christ and **gave us the ministry of reconciliation**." 2 Corinthians 5:18.

The Body of Christ, and each believer in particular, has been given the privilege and responsibility to call people to Christ. The last few verses in the Bible end with this ministry:

> The Spirit and the bride say, "Come." And let the one who hears say, "Come." And let the one who is thirsty come; let the one who wishes take the water of life without cost. Revelation 22:17.

What a beautiful ministry, to be used by the Spirit of Christ, to call people into fellowship with Him.

I am still pursuing the subject of "faith works by love." Love is the great motivator in the universe. It was love that sent Jesus to the cross. Perhaps the best-known verse in the Bible is this: "For God so loved the world, that He gave His only begotten Son." John 3:16. Maybe this should be the second best-known verse: "And **gave us the ministry of reconciliation**" 2 Corinthians 5:18. This capsulizes the Great Commission; however, the driving force should be faith working by love.

Jesus said on that last night, "If you love Me, you will keep My commandments" John 14:15. Then, just after the resurrection, He gave the apostles a powerful commandment: "Jesus came up and spoke to them, saying, 'All authority has been given to Me in heaven and on earth. Go therefore and make disciples of all the nations'" Matthew 28:18–19.

The great motivator to go should be our love for Christ. The great drawing force should be our love for the people we are calling. "I drew them with bands of love, the cords of a man."

Through a lack of love for God and for people, have you not used these promises and left them there idle? Some of you can say with Paul as he recounted what Jesus had said to him, **"So, King Agrippa, I did not prove disobedient to the heavenly vision"** Acts 26:19. If you have not been able to say that, repentance and a new decision are just a breath away.

THE POWER OF UNBELIEF

How can I talk with you about unbelief? What would touch our hearts and minds to abandon unbelief? Unbelief is everywhere. It pervades our culture, many of our churches, many of our leaders. It seems impervious to examples of God's love, to God's works, to miracles, to almost everything. It seems as resistant as steel. It seems to reign over faith; it seems more powerful even than love. It seems to feed the roots of our lives. It appears to be the ground that we grow in, what nurtures us. It almost seems invincible. It appears to be the most powerful force in the universe. Who can overcome it?

If the greatest of those born to women could not overcome it, what chance have I?

> I say to you, among those born of women there is no one greater than John the Baptist. Luke 7:28.

John had witnessed the following:

> Now when all the people were baptized, Jesus was also baptized, and while He was praying, heaven was opened, and the Holy Spirit descended upon Him in bodily form like a dove, and a voice came out of heaven, "You are My Beloved Son, in You I am well-pleased." Luke 3:21–22.

John had seen the Spirit descend upon Jesus and had heard God the Father speak audibly from heaven, witnessing that He was the Son of God. But when John had been put in prison, after a while, he began to doubt if Jesus was the Son of God or not. So he sent messengers to Jesus: "Summoning two of his disciples, John sent them to the Lord, saying, 'Are You the Expected One, or do we look for someone else?'" Luke 7:19. John is now filled with doubt.

One of Satan's greatest purposes is to make us doubt what God has said.

> The LORD God commanded the man, saying, "From any tree of the garden you may eat freely; but from the tree of the knowledge of good and evil you shall not eat, for in the day that you eat from it you will surely die." Genesis 2:16–17.

"The serpent said to the woman, 'You surely will not die!'" Genesis 3:4. She doubted God and believed the devil, and sin entered the world.

Satan tried this same trick with Jesus. Just prior to the forty days of trial, Jesus had been baptized, and that is when He heard the voice from heaven saying, "You are My Beloved Son." But Satan came to Him, testing Him. "And the tempter came and said to Him, 'If You are the Son of God, command that these stones become bread.'" Matthew 4:3. He was trying to create doubt about what the Father had said by saying, "If you are," prove it to me. He did this three times that day, and each time Jesus refused to prove who He was. He just lived who He was.

What is Satan challenging you to doubt? He knows that it is key to destroying your faith.

The noun "faith" is *pistis* in Greek; "unbelief" is *apistia.* In Greek usually a word preceded by "a" means without or non. It is like how "theist" means believing in God and "atheist" means without belief in God. So doubt is really without faith or unbelieving.

The impact of doubt is enormous. Look at what happened in Nazareth when Jesus visited.

"And He could do no miracle there except that He laid His hands on a few sick people and healed them. And He wondered at their unbelief." Mark 6:5–6.

He could do no miracle there. Unbelief has the power to stop Jesus from doing great things. How potent! Do we treat doubt in our lives lightly? Listen to what the writer of Hebrews said: "Take care, brethren, that there not be in any one of you an evil, unbelieving heart that falls away from the living God" Hebrews 3:12.

An "evil heart"? How disturbing. He goes on to say that the prime reason for the children of Israel not entering the promised land was not some great sin; rather, it was unbelief. "So we see that they were not able to enter because of unbelief." Hebrews 3:19. Has God promised you something that you cannot enter into because of unbelief?

There is help for our unbelief. Coming to Jesus is always an option. "Immediately the boy's father cried out and said, 'I do believe; help my unbelief.'" Mark 9:24.

The Power of Faith

As we believe God in prayer, we honor and please Him. "And without faith it is impossible to please *Him*, for he who comes to God must believe that He is and *that* He is a rewarder of those who seek Him." Hebrews 11:6.

By believing what He says, we honor Him. Our stepping out by faith in His promises when we pray delights Him. It says that He is trustworthy. We exalt Him by trusting Him. All through the Scriptures, God calls our attention to people who believe Him. Our faith not only exalts God; it also dethrones Satan and proves him a liar.

> The LORD said to Satan, "Have you considered My servant Job? For there is no one like him on the earth, a blameless and upright man, fearing God and turning away from evil." Job 1:8.
>
> Satan said, "But put forth Your hand now and touch all that he has; he will surely curse You to Your face." Job 1:11.

After Satan had taken all of Job's wealth and caused the deaths of his sons and daughters, Job proved Satan to be a liar. "Then Job arose and tore his robe and shaved his head, and he fell to the ground and worshiped." Job 1:20. The life of Job proved Satan to be a liar. Faith in the Lord in time of great trouble causes great honor to God.

God points out Abraham to us and what his faith means to God Himself. "Yet, with respect to the promise of God, he did not waver in unbelief but grew strong in faith, **giving glory to God**." Romans 4:20.

In the Gospels, Jesus occasionally points out people's good works, but His emphasis is constantly on people's faith. He points out people's need for faith by telling them that they have "little faith" or by pointing out results that came to them through faith. He at times exclaims that someone had "great faith":

> Then Jesus said to her, "O woman, your faith is great; it shall be done for you as you wish." And her daughter was healed at once. Matthew 15:28.

He makes this statement in response to a mother's persistent request that He heal her daughter. It was an example of Jesus's teaching that we should ask and keep on asking.

Most of us want to honor Jesus because He has done so much for us. A Roman centurion gave Jesus much honor by believing that Jesus could heal his servant without even being there. He believed that all that Jesus had to do was just give a commandment to have the servant healed, and it would be done. Jesus really responded to that faith:

> Now when Jesus heard *this*, He marveled and said to those who were following, "Truly I say to you, I have not found such great faith with anyone in Israel." Matthew 8:10.

He rewarded that faith by doing what was requested of Him.

In conclusion, we see that Jesus has given us repeated promises of what He would do if we were to believe and use these promises for the purposes they were given. God gives to humans opportunity to be used to transform our world, but He does not force us to do this. Some people walk away from His offers, and some walk into them. He gives you the choice. The destiny of how impacting your life will be lies in your hands, not God's. He makes success and powerful impact available to all, but only those who decided to step out on His promises will experience them. Twelve disciples were in the boat when Jesus came by walking on the water. Only one took the initiative to ask him if he could join Him out on the water. The other eleven watched Peter as he climbed out of the boat and walked on water to be with Jesus. Will you be one to risk it, or do you prefer to stay safely in the boat and miss the adventure of your life? If your life has no adventure, don't blame God. He has offered to make the impact of your life astounding. Review the promises of this chapter and the great offers by God. I challenge you to join the great adventure!

Jesus, may you be honored as we believe and use your promises for your glory.

6

The Rest of Believing

And to whom did He swear that they would not enter His rest, but to those who were disobedient? So we see that they were not able to enter because of unbelief. Hebrews 3:18–19

Therefore, let us fear if, while a promise remains of entering His rest, any one of you may seem to have come short of it. Hebrews 4:1.

So there remains a Sabbath rest for the people of God. For the one who has entered His rest has himself also rested from his works, as God did from His. Hebrews 4:9–10.

So there remains a Sabbath rest for the people of God. This Sabbath rest is a daily, moment-by-moment rest, not a rest of going to church on Sunday. It is a rest from our own works, a rest of believing. It says here that they were not able to enter this rest because of unbelief. There remains a rest of prayer, a rest believing God—that God has heard and will go to work. It is resting from self-effort.

My wife and I have been called by God to a ministry of "Go therefore and make disciples of all nations." It is a reproductive ministry. "Teaching them to observe all that I commanded you." What did he command us? "Go therefore and make disciples of all nations." What we do, they must likewise do. That is reproduction.

Is this commission to be carried out by self-effort? That would be how to work yourself to death. Could this be carried out by the rest of faith?

I had embraced this commission from Christ when I was about twenty years old. When I was twenty-five, while having a half day alone with God at Glen Eyrie, the headquarters of the Navigators, God spoke to me very clearly through the Bible. He initiated a promise that He wanted to give to me. I was not asking him for anything at the time. I was just worshipping and reading. He presented me with this:

> For when God made the promise to Abraham, since He could swear by no one greater, He swore by Himself, saying, "I WILL SURELY BLESS YOU AND I WILL SURELY MULTIPLY YOU." Hebrews 6:13–14.

God gave me this promise that said He would bless and multiply me, that He would fulfill this reproductive great commission ministry that He was giving me.

I, at that moment (and in subsequent years), believed that promise. I had climbed up a cliff to get this time alone. As I looked down, I thought, *If I trip and fall on my way back down and break my neck, God will still find a way to bring this to pass. It does not depend on my living but on His faithfulness.*

From that day on, I had a rest of faith. I believed that God would bring it to pass. Self-effort was not how it would be accomplished. Yes, I did need to obey Him day by day, but not in dependence on my efforts.

Curiously enough, on that same day, I was to later learn, God gave the identical promise to a young girl whom I was to later marry! We labored together in this reproductive commission from God, knowing that God would enable us and that we could rest in Him, believing He would fulfill that promise. The rest of faith says that I will obey God and walk with Him, but success is guaranteed beforehand. I don't have to strive to make it happen. It is like walking toward a goal that is already accomplished, although there are times when I forget and strive and worry.

You may not get the same promise from God, and you may not need it. You can live by the promises that God offers everyone in the opening verses of this chapter.

John 15 is a tremendous passage for rest and productivity. In verse 1, the Father is called the Vinedresser. He is the one responsible for making the vineyard productive. He prunes and shapes the vines to get the maximum harvest. Jesus is the Vine, so the vine is the best there is. The Vinedresser is God, and He is the best there is. A great harvest is expected.

Somehow in this teaching, the branches have a responsibility that is not normal. In a normal vine, the branches are an integral part of the vine and just exist and receive the sap from the roots and trunk of the vine. In the example that Jesus gave in John 15, these branches have the ability to remain (abide) in the vine or not. He exhorts them to stay connected to Jesus and states that Jesus plans to stay connected to them. If not, they will not bear grapes.

The reason He gives to encourage them to stay connected is that if they do not, they will be fruitless and useless. He says that if we abide in Jesus, and if His words abide in us, prayer becomes a resource for anything we desire—that is, our lives to become fruitful. We are connected to God in the right way, and as our prayers ascend, the answers descend. Notice that there are two important issues: Jesus and his teachings.

A few years ago, people were encouraged to live their lives asking the question: What Would Jesus Do (WWJD)? It lost its impact because people were not connected to the teachings and example of Jesus's life, and they did not know what Jesus would do. Stay connected to Jesus, and stay attached to His word. Let the person of Jesus abide in you, and let the words of Jesus abide in you. The written words of Jesus will keep you from straying to weird concepts of who Jesus is and what He would do.

> My Father is glorified by this, that you bear much fruit, and *so* prove to be My disciples. John 15:8.

This rest of faith in Jesus and His word is a rest of believing that the Father, as our vinedresser, will take care of us in such a way that we become very fruitful. I spend much of my time with believers to help them to Christ-likeness. Do you know what I have discovered? Most of them have an innate disposition to believe that God will *not* make them very fruitful. It is what He promises, but for them it is unbelievable.

Why is it so unbelievable that we would become very fruitful? I am not sure, but it seems to me that we often believe that God only rewards self-effort. We seem to believe that if we work hard at bearing fruit, we will be fruitful. To just rest in Jesus, the Vine, seems insufficient. But that idea is contrary to Jesus's teaching in John 15. He realizes that this very human tendency exists in us, so He makes the very clear statement and admonition to the Twelve:

> Abide in Me, and I in you. As the branch cannot bear fruit of itself unless it abides in the vine, so neither *can* you unless you abide in Me. I am the vine, you are the branches; he who abides in Me and I in him, he bears much fruit, for **apart from Me you can do nothing**. John 15:4–5.

What a beautiful teaching. Abiding in Him is the answer, not self-effort. Oh, if we could just believe this teaching, what joy would fill our hearts! I am obligated to repeat the opening verses in this chapter for your benefit.

> And to whom did He swear that they would not enter His rest, but to those who were disobedient? So we see that they were not able to enter because of unbelief. Hebrews 3:18–19.

> Therefore, let us fear if, while a promise remains of entering His rest, any one of you may seem to have come short of it. Hebrews 4:1.

> So there remains a Sabbath rest for the people of God. For the one who has entered His rest has himself also rested from his works, as God did from His. Hebrews 4:9–10.

Meditate on these verses and let them sink into your heart in all their fullness. The Apostle Paul wrote a short letter to the Philippian church with a theme of joy. He sums up His advice: "I can do all **things through Him who strengthens me**." Philippians 4:13.

Jesus wants to be our joy, our rest, our provision, our glory, our beauty, and our fruitfulness. "Abide in Me."

The title of this chapter is "The Rest of Believing." There is a verb, to believe: ***pisteuô***. The noun for this verb is "faith," ***pistis***. A noun is a person, place, or thing. A verb is an action; it is active and living. A study of the Gospel of John reveals something very interesting: John never uses the word "faith," only the verb "believe." Now the noun "faith" is a wonderful word and is used all over the Bible. But John is trying to communicate something special by using the verb, an active and living thing. You may have a Bible translation that translates this verb, "to believe," in John by using the phrase "put their faith in Him," but it is more simply and correctly translated, "believed in Him."

The rest of believing is an active rest. It is a constant thing. It is like the concept "abide in me." Just stay attached to Jesus. The branch is always attached; if not, it surely dies.

As John continues to write using this verb everywhere, we see this same concept of active rest.

> Now on the last day, the great *day* of the feast, Jesus stood and cried out, saying, "If anyone is thirsty, let him come to Me and drink. He who believes in Me, as the Scripture said, 'From his innermost being will flow rivers of living water.'" But this He spoke of the Spirit, whom those who believed in Him were to receive; for the Spirit was not yet *given*, because Jesus was not yet glorified. John 7:37–39.

When he says, "He who believes in Me," people often think only of their coming to faith in Christ. But I suspect that He is speaking of a moment-by-moment trust, walking with Him and expecting that out of our beings will constantly be flowing rivers of living water. I know many believers who have a dry, parched life as a regular experience. But if we are submitting to Christ as Lord on a continual basis, we can and should expect living waters to be flowing from us wherever we go during the day each day. I often remind the Lord as I drive somewhere that I am expecting flowing rivers to be happening.

As I have meditated on this passage, I have come to realize that I cannot make these rivers flow; that is the task of the Spirit. I will experience them flowing as I believe Him to bring this to pass. But I ask myself, what is my part? I cannot make them flow; that is God's task. However, I think I can stop the flow by disobedience or by unbelief. Many believers do not experience this flow, as they lead dry lives, and I suspect these two issues stop this generous flow of the Spirit: disobedience or unbelief.

Do you believe this passage? If so, start expecting these rivers to flow, and they will. I have learned to not tell God what the result should be. Just let them flow, and like around any good spring of water, green things will spring up. Let me mention here that Jesus says it will not be one river, but *rivers*. Multiple things will be happening. What an exciting and productive life in the Spirit is promised to those who will be living believing. Once again, this is the active rest of faith.

Jesus approaches this idea in another way:

> Come to Me, all who are weary and heavy-laden, and I will give you rest. Take My yoke upon you and learn from Me, for I am gentle and humble in heart, and YOU WILL FIND REST FOR YOUR SOULS, for My yoke is easy and My burden is light. Matthew 11:28–30.

We can come to Jesus in fellowship (prayer) daily. As we sit in His presence, weary and heavy with our burdens, Jesus joins us, His presence is with us (often unperceived), and He makes an exchange. He takes what is burdensome to us and gives us His light burden. In His burden, our soul comes to rest. Is it a heavy burden to love the unlovely? Is it heavy to share His love for them? Does it in reality give you delight to make known the lover of our souls?

Last night my wife and I sat at a dinner table with two friends who had no idea how to gain assurance of eternal life. They quietly listened as we shared our journey to find life in Christ. They did not immediately respond to Christ's invitation. But we can rest in Him, for we cannot make them believe and receive. That is too heavy a burden for us. It is the one Christ wants to carry. Even He shifts this burden to the Father: "All that the Father gives Me will come to Me, and the one who comes to Me I will certainly not cast out" John 6:37. Can we rest trusting the Father?

If your soul is in turmoil for yourself or others, it will come to rest only as you believe that He is the lover of your soul and of theirs. Place them or yourself in His hands or rest under His wings, as the palmist says: "He who dwells [or abides] in the shelter of the Most High Will abide in the shadow of the Almighty. I will say to the LORD, 'My refuge and my fortress, My God, in whom I trust!'" Psalm 91:1–2. Abiding is not a New Testament concept. It is a relationship with God and Christ. Trust Him with your life and theirs.

There is another rest of believing. It is the rest of believing praise and believing thanksgiving. Praise has more to do with who God is and what He has promised, and thanksgiving has more to do with what God has done and how He has treated us.

I say believing praise, for it is what you really believe about Him, not what we have learned we should say about Him. I really believe God is my Father. In prayer, I praise Him that He gave a new birth to my spirit. I worship Him for who He is and for what he has made me become. I am a son (many of you are daughters) of the Highest.

I am a father to a son and two daughters. I actually have two sons and three daughters. Figure it out. I have one married son and one married daughter. In my heart there is a special relationship to all five. I avoid thinking "daughter-in-law" or "son-in-law." I always sign off my e-mails to them, "Dad."

I would like to leave a thought with you, ladies. Think of yourselves in a special way, not as sons of God but as daughters. Being a father of both, I recognize that, emotionally, I have one emotion toward my sons and another emotion toward my daughters. I love each of them equally, I believe, but not in the same way. Boys have a special masculine attachment to their father, but my girls have a special feminine attachment in my psyche. Is God the same? I would encourage you to think of yourself as God's daughters.

I love going fishing with my son, though he doesn't like fishing. But going stream fishing with my daughter leaves something special that is unlike fishing with my son. Ladies, when you look up into the eyes of your heavenly Father, see the special insight He has for your femininity. He created it.

Moving on to other aspects of believing praise, on many issues we can go from asking to praising.

Do you ask God to be with you? But He has promised to be with you. "I WILL NEVER DESERT YOU, NOR WILL I EVER FORSAKE YOU." Hebrews 13:5. Instead of asking for Him to be with you, why not honor Him by thanking Him that He will always be with you?

Do you ask God to guide you? "But when He, the Spirit of truth, comes, He will guide you into all the truth." John 16:13. Knowing this promise, can you trust Him to guide you and praise Him for that fact that he promises to guide you? Look at Proverbs 3:5–6: "Trust in the LORD with all your heart. And do not lean on your own understanding. In all your ways acknowledge Him, And He will make your paths straight." Instead, say, "Lord, I acknowledge that my own understanding is not where I should put my trust. I trust you and praise you that as I trust in your guidance that you promise to guide me into a good path. Lord, I rest in your guidance."

Do you beg God to keep you from temptation, or can you thank God that He will be faithful to rescue you?

> No temptation has overtaken you but such as is common to man; and God is faithful, who will not allow you to be tempted beyond what you are able, but with the temptation will provide the way of escape also, so that you will be able to endure it. 1 Corinthians 10:13.

Search through the Word of God for promises that He has already given to us and use them for resting in Him and for praising Him. He is honored as you choose to trust in what He has declared that He will do for you already.

There is rest for a troubled heart. Sometimes chapter breaks that are inserted in the Bible mask some truths for us. The Bible was not written with verse and chapter breaks. The chapter divisions commonly used today were developed by Stephen Langton, an archbishop of Canterbury. Langton put the modern chapter divisions into place in around AD 1227. Often they are a help; at other times they are not.

We all are familiar with the saying of Jesus, "Do not let your heart be troubled; believe in God, believe also in Me." John 14:1. Are you familiar with why He said it? The verses that immediately precede it are assigned to the previous chapter, but the end of chapter 13 belongs to chapter 14: "Peter said to Him, Lord, why can I not follow You right now? I will lay down my life for You."

Jesus answered, "Will you lay down your life for Me? Truly, truly, I say to you, a rooster will not crow until you deny Me three times." Then Jesus says, "Do not let your heart be troubled." Jesus says to Peter that it will happen but that God will use it for good later on. In the second half of this verse, He says to Peter, "You trust in God, now trust in Me."

The rest of believing prayer and praise *before an event occurs* honors God in a special way. Before King Jehoshaphat experiences this rest, comes a heart searching before God. He was facing an invasion by a large army and recognized that if God did not help them they would be defeated.

> O our God, will You not judge them? For we are powerless before this great multitude who are coming against us; nor do we know what to do, but our eyes are on You. All Judah was standing before the LORD, with their infants, their wives and their children. 2 Chronicles 20:12–13.

It is especially touching that they gathered all the babies and little children before God.

In response to their seeking God, a prophet told them, "You *need* not fight in this *battle*; station yourselves, stand and see the salvation of the LORD on your behalf." 2 Chronicles 20:17.

They believed this word from God, and:

> When he had consulted with the people, he appointed those who sang to the LORD and those who praised *Him* in holy attire, as they went out **before the army** and said, "Give thanks to the LORD, for His lovingkindness is everlasting." **When they began singing and praising**, the LORD set ambushes against the sons of Ammon, Moab and Mount Seir, who had come against Judah; so they were routed. 2 Chronicles 20:21–22

Praise in some situations is more effective than petition. When in college in San Diego, I had a Sunday School teacher who was a prayer warrior. When she was a young married woman, her husband became bedridden and was very sick. Nothing seemed to help. She had to earn their living as a nurse. They had almost no money and no car, so she was forced to walk to the hospital, which was about an hour and a half away. Walking to and from work, over a period of three to four weeks, she spent the three hours daily asking God for help, but the situation did not change.

One day she encountered a missionary lady who advised her to stop asking and to spend the time in praise. She then spent the three hours daily in praise. A very short time after that, their situation was resolved.

As I review this chapter, three things call my attention:

1. **What upsets you?**

Are you upset often about a reoccurring theme? Do you lie awake at night worrying over something? You need a new pattern in your life—the rest of faith. Have you given up hope on breaking a lifelong pattern and establishing a new life of rest? If so, recognize this hopelessness as unbelief. We must understand the seriousness of unbelief. God calls an unbelieving heart evil. "Take care, brethren, that there not be in any one of you an evil, unbelieving heart" Hebrews 3:12.

Confess to God that your heart is evil. Confession brings cleansing. Ask Him to establish a new pattern for you, a rest of faith. A friend of mine where we are living will turn ninety-three in just a few days. She was lying awake at night, worrying. I told her what I do when this happens to me. I review Philippians 4:6–7:

> Be anxious for nothing, but in everything by prayer and supplication with thanksgiving let your requests be made known to God, and the peace of God, which surpasses all comprehension, will guard your hearts and your minds in Christ Jesus.

Being ninety-two, she found memorizing these two verses difficult. But she worked at it every day. She is experiencing the rest of peace and can quote these verses from memory now as she is lying in bed with the lights out.

To change a lifelong pattern, we must see the present pattern as a very serious problem. God helps us see the seriousness of an unbelieving heart by calling it evil. He wants to motivate us to leave a life of unbelief for a life of faith.

Changing a long-term pattern is possible. It happened to me this month. About six weeks ago, while exercising, I had A-fib, heart fibrillation. I went right away to my cardiologist. In reviewing my records, she found that I have sleep apnea and a CPAP machine to help me breathe at night. I was in the habit of taking off the mask and shutting down the machine at about 2:00 a.m., getting up for two or three hours, and not using it the rest of the night. This had been going on for about fifteen years.

She said this might be the cause of my A-fib and that I needed to leave the machine on all night, about eight hours. If not, I would be susceptible to a stroke. The results of staying with my old habit could be disastrous.

That night I decided to follow her instructions. Not a night since have I had it on for less than seven or eight hours. I am sure that God is helping me to do the right thing. Changing long-term habits can be done with God's help and a committed decision.

2. Springs of living water. John 7:37–39.

Can you expect springs of living water to flow out from you to bless those whom you encounter? This promise is one of what God will do through you for others. It is outreach. Will you make a decision to believe this promise of Christ and to actively trust Him *each day* to flow through you wherever you are? Choose to enter this experience of joy and blessing through faith in this declaration of Jesus.

3. A very fruitful life. John 15

This third option of faith in the operation of abiding in the Vine is a challenge for you to believe in His graciousness. Will you choose to enter the joy of bringing great glory to the Father by the active faith of abiding and believing that He is able to make your life a very fruitful branch? The promise is for you, but you must choose to believe it.

Any one or all three points are available to you if you choose to trust in these promises from God Himself. May God give you a believing heart and a life filled with usefulness.

7

Understand God's Purposes for Heaven and Earth

To guide us into asking what is consistent with what is on God's heart, we need to understand His purposes. By this we will be praying in God's will.

In this chapter I am not trying to do a theological thesis. I am trying to help you as an intercessor to connect with the heart of God.

- **Jesus came to seek and save the lost.**

This sentence sounds so much like a well-thought-through mission statement that someone might sign his or her name to in order to join an organization. What did this statement mean to Jesus?

Let me give you an illustration. If you order ham and eggs for breakfast, it is a harmless statement on a menu. What will it cost the chicken to provide the eggs? It will cost her very little. What will it cost the pig to provide the ham? It will cost him his life.

What did the statement "Jesus came to seek and save the lost" cost Jesus and the disciples? Why did Jesus sweat great drops of blood at Gethsemane? Why did Peter, in fear, deny Jesus that night? Why did all the apostles run away? Why did Jesus find them three days later in a room with the door locked?

> Later on that day, the disciples had gathered together, but, fearful of the Jews, had locked all the doors in the house. Jesus entered, stood among them, and said, "Peace to you." John 20:19 (MSG).

What did it cost the Father to abandon His Son on the cross? Something unimaginable and inexplicable.

What will the assimilation of this statement into our lives cost us? It will be different for each of us, but not cheap.

What will it cost the lost? "Repent and believe" is the message. The price has been paid; salvation is offered freely.

- **All believers, those He brings to salvation, would become united as one.**

As a large family, we would be undivided in love and the unity of the universal Body of Christ. As a body, we would individually live a Christlike life, one that would glorify our Father in heaven.

- **As one body, we are commissioned to bring Christlikeness to the lost world.**

Collectively and individually we are termed "ambassadors" of God to call the world to repentance, faith, and Christlikeness.

There is a strange thing about most of Christianity. Many pastors and church leaders would not only affirm the above paragraph but also preach those concepts. The strange phenomenon is that those who sit in the pews listening to these beautiful truths seem to give assent to them but often are unmoved to personally become ambassadors.

I have no solution for this inertia.

This week a regular church-attending believer I know wrote to me the following:

> *"I asked God over and over for Him to reveal Himself to me in a way that I can understand so that I grow and experience more of what a Christian should. I don't want to be a normal or nominal Christian anymore. Why? They have small faith with few answers to prayer and don't experience the joy of God working in their lives. Most Christians I know are like this."*

I have no indictment against the Christian church and only share what he is feeling as a sample of what seems to be happening. You will have to work your way through this and ask yourself if you are sitting and watching or actively participating in this great mission. If you are concerned about yourself, try praying as the person who wrote the above quote is praying for himself.

- **We believe in the individuality of each believer, each with his or her individual abilities, gifting, and purpose in Christ.**

Each believer has a unique value in the sight of God, the same as each child in a family is precious in who he or she is. We each are endowed by the Spirit with a gift or multiple spiritual gifts with which to serve the Kingdom of God and the Body of Christ. These do not seem to be easily identified. I say this because when I ask a normal churchgoing believer what his or her spiritual gift or gifts are, he or she looks mystified and has no answer.

I stated: "each with his or her individual abilities, gifting, and purpose in Christ." Along with often not being aware of their spiritual gift, believers seem similarly unaware of their individual purpose. Paul in Romans talks about the "gifts and calling of God." The calling is a purpose. Everywhere I go I try to inspire the young and old alike to look to God for some communication from Him about their purpose in life.

God has spoken to both my wife and me about a purpose in life. We have been following that for the past fifty-nine years. Some people choose a life purpose for themselves, but we often counsel people to seek some kind of indication from God. You will be more sure that you are pursuing the right goal by listening to Him in His Word. If you have lived your life without a calling from God, it is never too late to ask Him for clear direction. His calling will be in line with your spiritual gifting. My wife and I have the same calling but different and complementary gifting.

Our calling came in stages. First, through the Navigators, we believed we should be giving our lives to make disciples who would become reproductive—that is, disciples who would make disciples with a vision to reproduce their Christlikeness in another, and that that person would do the same with another, and so on and on, a chain reaction. This conviction came through Christ's commission to the more than five hundred disciples in Galilee after His resurrection. He told them to go into all the world and make disciples of all the nations. In making these disciples, He said that they must teach them all that they had learned from Him. One of the things that they had learned from Him was to go and make disciples and to teach others to do the same.

So, our purpose came right from the mouth of Jesus.

The second stage of our calling was given to us some five or six years later in our time alone with Jesus in the Bible. He gave us a promise that He would multiply our lives—that is, reproductive disciples: "Saying, 'I WILL SURELY BLESS YOU AND I WILL SURELY MULTIPLY YOU.'" Hebrews 6:14.

From that time on, we lived knowing that God would fulfill our purpose. We had only to obey Him day after day, trusting in Him to bring about the results.

Purpose puts action into our lives. The Apostle Paul said:

> Brethren, I do not regard myself as having laid hold of it yet; but one thing I do: forgetting what lies behind and reaching forward to what lies ahead, **I press on toward the goal** for the prize of the upward call of God in Christ Jesus. Philippians 3:13–14.

Purpose allows me to press on toward something.

I have a major goal but also a couple of other goals. One of my goals or purposes is more effective praying for myself. Another is to stimulate others to effective prayer. To this end, I am writing this book.

I feel helpless to give you a purpose. I can pray for you to come to find a purpose for your life as a believer. But there must be something within you or within the Word of God or from the Spirit of God to drive you to find a purpose,

What drove me to write this chapter was an article from a fourteen-year-old girl. With permission, her mother let me read the statement of faith that her daughter had written as a result of confirmation in a Lutheran church. The statement was beautiful and in her own words. I looked through it and could find no way to improve it. I would be honored for one of my granddaughters to write a statement of faith like that.

As I meditated on what she wrote, I realized that she needed an accompanying statement of purpose, something that would mobilize her life. She needed a vision of what to do with this faith.

That is what Dawson Trotman, the founder of the Navigators, gave to me at age eighteen: a great vision of what to do with my life based on God's Word. It had to do with the Great Commission of Christ to His disciples and to all future disciples in Matthew 28.

I encouraged this mother to ask her daughter to write a corresponding paper on purpose. I am eager to see what she comes up with. Why don't you do the same and give it to someone who has purpose in his or her life to read and comment on? Pray as you write it. Ask the Spirit of God to enlighten you and to guide you.

If you need some additional help, I have written a book titled *Disciple Making for a New Generation* that you can get on Amazon.com. Read chapter 1, "A Vision and a Commission Worthy of a Lifetime Pursuit," and chapter 2, "Getting Started in the Right Direction and Know Where You Are Going." Another book that might help is *The Purpose Driven Life* by Rick Warren.

- **Two people came to me this month. One said, "How can I be saved?" The other said, "Would you mentor me in the Christian life?"**

The first wanted to enter into eternal life, to be saved, and to live in heaven when this earthly life is over.

The second wanted to live an eternally meaningful life during his time on earth, having already secured a place in heaven.

I am awed by a sense of the privilege to be a pathfinder for both of these people.

For the first, to populate the heavens with sons and daughters of God.

For the second, to populate the earth with people who live an eternally meaningful life during their journey here. To leave people who can leave a legacy of generations of godly people upon the earth—what a privilege I have been given!

God's design is for His children to produce a "bountiful harvest" of people in both of these categories. Jesus said, "My true disciples produce bountiful harvests. This brings great glory to my Father." John 15:8 (TLB).

Imagine: you and many others bringing "great glory" to the Father!

God guided me over a period of some years to write two books. The first was a pathfinder for the people who ask, "How can I be saved?" The title is: *What If God Exists?*

The second is a pathfinder for people who want what the second asked, "Would you mentor me?" It is *Disciple Making for a New Generation: Leaving a Legacy of Generations of Godly Men and Women.*

In the foreword of this book, a personal friend, Bill Tell, then senior vice-president and chief of staff of the Navigators, wrote, "To read this book is like spending time with a personal mentor, one with whom you cannot get enough time. By the time you have finished the last chapter, you have walked with Jack through fifty years of ministry and will have a new paradigm of what it means to 'make disciples.' You will have a glimpse of what it might look like in our day to not only pass on the truth of the gospel, but are to impart our very lives to the next generation."

Don't live another month without purpose; life is too short.

We must have a clear purpose, but that is only half of the story.

We must have the right *motive*.

We have all seen people with a strong purpose but with a flawed motive. Motives that center around self-fulfillment are poisonous. These motives destroy people around us. A mission accomplished with a wrong motive will not endure.

We have all known pastors and leaders who were driven to accomplish but left wrecked lives in their wake. They accomplished their goals but at what price to the people around them or to their families?

Before I give you a couple of examples of the results of purpose with a wrong motive, let me speak of the right motive.

What are God's and Jesus's motives?

Love.

I wrote of this characteristic in chapter 2 when speaking of the characteristics of God.

We know what motivated God to redeem people.

"**For God so loved the world,** that He gave His only begotten Son..."

So as God's representatives (i.e., ambassadors), we must carry on this mission with the same motive to be able to accurately represent Him. In the same passage where the Apostle Paul calls us ambassadors, he precedes it with this: "**For Christ's love compels us**, because we are convinced that one died for all, and therefore all died." 2 Corinthians 5:14 (NIV).

My first example of a person with a wrong motive is myself. At twenty-three years old and still a college student, I was appointed as temporary director of a Navigator training home by Dawson Trotman, the founder. I was filled with purpose and energy in evangelism and disciple making. But there was a problem that Dawson did not know about. One of the men under training called me "the whip." I was driven with purpose without love. I did not see this at the time, and I was very pleased with my life.

God saw this, and one morning in my quiet time and Bible reading, God spoke to me very severely.

> Because you say, "I am rich, and have become wealthy, and have need of nothing," and you do not know that *you are wretched and miserable and poor and blind and naked.* Revelation 3:17.

His view of me shook me to the core. I am not sure how I knew what my problem was, but I identified it as the need for love, God's type of love, redemptive love. I was purpose driven without love. I was the whip.

Seeing God's perspective of myself started me on a yearlong journey seeking love for my life. At the end of that year, I recognized that my life was now filled with God's love. If you want to read about this journey, it is in my book on disciple making in the chapter on the development of love in a disciple. It seems that this type of love comes only from God Himself. My key discoveries were in these passages by the Apostle Paul:

> May the Lord direct your hearts into the love of God and into the steadfastness of Christ. 2 Thessalonians 3:5.

> And the grace of our Lord was more than abundant, with the faith and love which are *found* in Christ Jesus. 1 Timothy 1:14.

This love comes to us by the grace of God. It is a gift. This love continues with me to this day, although it is still being perfected.

I often have trained college students. One girl whose father was a nationally known radio evangelist in a nation I will not name, related how she and her brother and mother suffered under this man. The whole family was very bitter against God for the father's neglect of them. Charging off with a great purpose and neglecting your family is not a good option.

In another church that Joann and I attended, there was a nationally famous Bible teacher whom we all admired. This Bible teacher passed away about six years later. I was on a ship traveling, and his son was there, too. I was shocked when he recounted that he was coming from his father's funeral, where he had stood up at his grave and announced to the crowd what a terrible father he had been. This young man was very angry at God.

A good purpose without love wrecks lives. The same purpose driven by love builds up the Kingdom of God.

8

Prevailing Prayer

THIS IS ONE of those beautiful chapters. It is a subject that offers great hope and immense rewards. It is the gateway to resolving difficult problems and of experiencing significant transformation. Are you or a loved one addicted to something—maybe sex, porn, gambling, drugs, anger, or selfishness? You may find some new hope here. Have you been facing some roadblocks in your life or ministry that you have been unable to overcome? You sense that if God does not step in, you are dead in the water. However, many times we are facing things that we need to step up and own to solve. I don't ask God to get me dressed or to fix lunch for me or to put in my hearing aids or to drive my car for me. Prevailing prayer is not asking God to do what we ought to do; it is asking God to do what we cannot do.

We need to differentiate between prevailing prayer and persevering prayer. Persevering prayer could be defined as something that you are asking but that is slow in coming. It is not giving up, but continually keeping it before the throne of God until the answer comes. It is taught by Jesus in Luke 18 in a parable about a widow and an unjust judge. The widow is motivated to get out of bed and to go to see the judge about her case. She is totally unable to do his job, which is to decide her case.

Prevailing prayer is somewhat different; it is exemplified by Jacob's wrestling with God and by the Syrophoenician woman who kept after

Jesus in his initial refusal to her request until it was granted. **Prevailing prayer is having an important issue that needs to be solved.** It is very important and may require spending a few minutes or several hours in prayer until God decides finally to grant your request. It may appear that God is reluctant, but often there is another reason that only extended time in prayer may reveal.

Sometimes it is us wrestling with God, and other times it will become apparent that it is God wrestling with us.

Genesis 32

The background with Jacob and Esau is that Esau vowed to kill his brother Jacob some years earlier. Realizing this, Jacob's mother sent him away to a far land to find a wife. Jacob goes, and years pass during which he gets two wives. Between them and their maidservants, he has twelve sons who later are called the twelve tribes of Israel. He then returns to his home country after more than twenty years of absence. Chapter 32 describes this attempt.

Jacob is filled with fear that Esau still holds a grudge and may try to annihilate him, his wives, and his children. He attempts to appease his brother with great gifts that he sends on before him. The messengers that he sends to Esau come back reporting that Esau **is coming with four hundred men to meet him**. This news of a small army coming puts Jacob in a panic, confirming his belief that Esau is planning to kill them all. Jacob has no army by which to defend himself. He now looks to God to save him.

He reminds God that he is returning to his homeland because God told him to. Jacob says,

> O God of my father Abraham and God of my father Isaac, O LORD, who said to me, "Return to your country and to your relatives, and I will prosper you…" Genesis 32:9.

He sends all his wives, children, and possessions on before him and stays alone, beseeching God to protect him and his family. He wrestles all night, until daybreak, with a man who apparently is an angel. The angel wants to leave at daybreak, but Jacob hangs on, saying he will not let loose of him until he pronounces a blessing on Jacob so that he and his family will not be destroyed. Then the angel says,

> "Let me go, for the dawn is breaking." But Jacob says, "I will not let you go unless you bless me." Genesis 32:26.
>
> The angel says, "Your name shall no longer be Jacob, but Israel; **for you have striven with God and with men and have prevailed.** Genesis 32:28.

That morning he meets Esau, who accepts an appeasement offering from Jacob, and disaster is averted.

I mentioned that sometimes we wrestle with God, and sometimes God is wrestling with us. In the verse above, the angel asks him about his name, and he must admit what type of person he is. Jacob and Esau were born twins, and they were fighting in the womb. Esau was born first and is considered the firstborn, but Jacob came out of the womb holding onto his brother's heel.

God had revealed to his mother that Jacob would prevail over Esau. Jacob steals his brother's blessing later on, which causes Esau to want to kill him. On birth he is named Jacob, which means "supplanter" or "trickster." He must admit to God that he has been that kind of person before God will save him and give him a new name, Israel. One translator defines Israel as "he fights or persists with God" (in prevailing prayer). The wrestling worked two ways.

This is a defining night for Jacob, as he is transformed from a trickster or one who makes deals to get his own way, into someone who prevails with God. God is now his savior, rather than his cleverness. Earlier, as Jacob was leaving the promised land to get a wife, he has a vision of God and a promise from God, but he has a long way to go spiritually. Here is his response to God:

"If God will be with me and will keep me on this journey that I take, and will give me food to eat and garments to wear, and I return to my father's house in safety, **then the LORD will be my God**. This stone, which I have set up as a pillar, will be God's house, and of all that You give me I will surely give a tenth to You." Genesis 28:20–22.

Jacob is bargaining with God that if God will take care of him, **then the LORD will be my God**. This is a conditional commitment to the Lord. He goes on to make another vow, or bargain: to return to the Lord 10 percent of what God gives him. Is he trying to buy off God?

This event touches me very much, for as a young Christian I manipulated people for my own ends. I had a very glib tongue. God revealed to me that manipulating people is very ungodly. I learned to trust in Him instead.

In the context of Genesis 32, prevailing prayer is clinging to God in prayer until He grants the request. This is not submissive praying; it is desperation praying, seeking God until we get an answer from Him. The net result of this wrestling with God is that Jacob gets very much more than what he is requesting. He gets his request for safety from his brother, *and* he is forever changed. His name is changed from Jacob—a supplanter or a bargainer—to Israel—a man who prevails with God and people. His personality is changed, and his God is no longer a provisional God. We do not know God's motive in that night of wrestling, but the angel dislocates Jacob's hip, and the muscle involved. Israel is given a permanent disability that will remind him for the rest of his life about this struggle. Unexpected things happen to us as we wrestle with God.

The Syrophoenician Woman

This is what happened in Matthew 15:21–22:

> Jesus went away from there, and withdrew into the district of Tyre and Sidon. And a Canaanite woman from that region came out and *began* to cry out, saying, "Have mercy on me, Lord, Son of David; my daughter is cruelly demon-possessed."

Jesus at first was silent and did not respond to her. She kept insisting that Jesus grant her request, so much so that the disciples begged Him to send her away because she kept shouting at them. "But she came and *began* to bow down before Him, saying, 'Lord, help me!'" Finally, after she argued with Jesus about His refusal, Jesus said, "O woman, your faith is great; it shall be done for you as you wish." And her daughter was healed at once. Matthew 15:28. This is the New Testament reflection of Jacob's situation. This is prevailing prayer.

I have found that sometimes I pray for something daily for a while, but the answer does not come. If it is really important, and I realize that my praying is not effectual, I set aside some time to be before God to inquire as to why the answer is not coming.

In this extended time, either my faith is strengthened or God reveals a wrong motive or some other issue that I need to resolve before the answer will come. I have seen real breakthroughs come to me and other people or ministries I have been praying for, as God wrestles with me about an obstacle in my own life or about my unbelief.

Sometimes God wants to see if we really want what we are asking for. Do we pray for a while, maybe a few weeks, and if no answer comes, we give up? Do we only want it if it is easy to obtain? The key seems to be in how deeply you desire something. The Apostle Paul did not take things lightly as he said, "My little children, of whom I travail in birth again until Christ be formed in you." Galatians 4:19 (KJV). Is this prevailing prayer?

Sometimes, after you wrestle with God over an issue, he may deny the request, as in the example of the Apostle Paul:

> Concerning this I implored the Lord three times that it might leave me. And He has said to me, "My grace is sufficient for you, for power is perfected in weakness." Most gladly, therefore, I will rather boast about my weaknesses, so that the power of Christ may dwell in me. 2 Corinthians 12:8–9.

In this case God had a purpose in Paul's suffering.

I think of the young man who came to Jesus, asking Him what he would need to do to gain eternal life.

> Jesus said to him, "If you wish to be complete, go *and* sell your possessions and give to *the* poor, and you will have treasure in heaven; and come, follow Me." But when the young man heard this statement, **he went away grieving; for he was one who owned much property**. Matthew 19:21–22.

The man did seem to want eternal life, for his desire for money exceeded his desire for eternal life. A lukewarm heart will betray us. As a result, we will not walk in the will of God but will walk in a tepid spiritual life before God.

Consider the lack of enthusiasm of Joash, the king of Israel in Samaria. Elisha was dying, and the king wanted a last blessing for the nation from Elisha, so the following happened:

> Then he [Elisha] said, "Take the arrows," and he [Joash] took them. And he said to the king of Israel, "Strike the ground," and he struck *it* three times and stopped. So the man of God was angry with him and said, "You should have struck five or six times, then you would have struck Aram until you would have destroyed *it.* But now you shall strike Aram *only* three times." 2 Kings 13:18–19.

The arrows and striking the ground were symbols of God defeating the king of Aram. God responded to the lack of enthusiasm of Joash by giving him only three victories over their battles. Elisha said that God would have utterly destroyed them if he had continued hitting the ground with them. God responds to people's attitudes, it seems.

Are you facing a serious issue of life or ministry that God might be willing to solve if you would seriously seek Him, as the Syrophoenician woman did? Spend time meditating on Matthew 15:21–28 to see the whole struggle she had with Jesus.

Even reading about Jacob's wrestling with God may bring new light to you. This type of prayer is not something that we do daily but on serious occasions, as with Jacob. As I look back over my life, I can recall three different occasions that called for this type of praying. It resulted in transformation for me and for other people with whom I was involved.

If you have a situation that may require this type of praying, here is a practical suggestion that you might want to consider. When I am faced with a prevailing prayer issue, because I don't know how long I will be in prayer, I pick a time when I have a large, open slot of time such as a whole afternoon. One time I picked a time when I was going to bed and could pray for several hours if necessary. Jacob did that. God may answer you in five minutes or in five hours.

I have talked with believers who have had a serious family situation. I thought that it might be solvable with some serious prayer before God. I offered to spend extended time in prayer before God with them. They could not see that this might help, and they did not accept my offer. They were church leaders but could not imagine that two or three hours before God might bring an answer and solution from God. The example of the Syrophoenician woman made no impression on them.

This may be a brand-new concept for you. What will you do with it? You will probably look at your life and ministry with new eyes. You may list the significant obstacles in your life or in the lives of people you love. You may become overwhelmed with this.

Probably the first thing that you will encounter is your little faith or your unbelief. Setting time aside to be with God and to open your heart to Him is the first step. Looking at God in the Word of God and at the promises of God will begin to bring healing to your unbelief and hope to your soul. Just sitting and looking at yourself will bring great discouragement. Do as David did; come and sit before God in helplessness and wonder.

The great prophet Elijah faced the wrath of Jezebel, who threatened to kill him. It was too much for him. He fled the county. He was exhausted and in the desert. As he was sleeping, as is recorded in 1 Kings 19, God sent an angel to provide food and water, let him sleep some more, woke him up again, and provided more food and water for him. God dealt with him tenderly. How will God not deal with you tenderly? He loves you deeply. Come to Him. "Come to Me, all who are weary and heavy-laden, and I will give you rest" Matthew 11:28.

I believe He will help you as you seek Him.

History records the cases of many people of prevailing prayer. In books about prayer, you will often read about the experiences of others, especially books about missionaries. There was a missionary to India about one hundred years ago, whose life is detailed in the book *Praying Hyde*. Another is *Behind the Ranges* by J. O. Fraser. These men experienced great breakthroughs where many people came to Christ as they persevered in prayer.

I just finished reading *Autobiography of Charles G. Finney*, printed 1876, which detailed his evangelistic efforts in the northeast from 1828 to 1875. During his ministry, it is estimated that about five hundred thousand came to Christ. God raised up many praying men and women to influence what was happening. The illustrations are numerous, but the following statement on page 297 is revealing:

> I know at the time a considerable number of men that were exercised in the same way [prevailing prayer]. A deacon P—— of Camden, Oneida county; a deacon T—— of Rodman, Jefferson county; a deacon B—— of Adams, in the same county; this Mr. Clary, and many others among the men, and a large number of women, partook of the same spirit, and spent a great part of their time in prayer. Father Nash, as we called him, who in several of my fields of labor came to me and aided me, was another of those men that has such a powerful spirit of prevailing prayer.

Finney recounts one of the results of that prevailing prayer on page 293:

> A revival took tremendous hold of that school [a high school in Rochester]. Mr. B—— (the principal) himself was soon hopefully converted, and nearly every person in the school. A few years since, Miss A—— informed me that more than forty persons in that school had become ministers. This was a fact that I had not known before. She named many of them to me at the time. A large number of them had become foreign missionaries.

I have been reluctant to share some of my own journey with prevailing prayer. This is partly because every person will have his or her own unique experience with God and should not attempt to duplicate another person's experience or journey. So whatever your journey becomes, I know it will be very different from mine.

What has encouraged me to write about mine is the fact that God saw fit to make public the amazing and unique journey of Jacob with all of its good, bad, and ugly features.

My God journey with prevailing prayer began in September 1964 in Germany, where we were working with American servicemen and women. I had been leading a ministry for almost two years. I had a great burden on my heart to lead people to Christ on three US air bases in my area. I was not succeeding according to my own evaluation. Some people were coming to Christ, but I felt it was a very minimal harvest. I am not sure how I arrived to the conclusion that God was the key to my dreams, but I was sure that He was.

Just about three weeks before my time in prayer, we had the astounding joy of the birth of our firstborn, Daniel. But along with this joy, my soul was troubled for lost people without my Savior whom I worshipped and enjoyed. Even though I loved my wife and child deeply, my soul was overwhelmed by the eternal lostness of others. I cannot explain how a man so blessed of God with this beautiful family could say to God that night, "I would rather die than to continue in this way of fruitlessness in bringing in the lost."

As I look back today, I can only conclude that God was somehow in this feeling of desperation.

It was about 9:00 p.m., and Joann was just going to sleep. I informed her that I would come to bed later and was going to pray awhile.

As I got on my knees with a Bible open before me, I told God that I would stay with Him in prayer until He answered my prayer or until I expired of hunger or thirst. Living without a solution was not an option.

As I cried out to God for His blessing, I began to feel abandoned by Him, even though I knew Hebrews 13:5, "I will never leave you nor forsake you."

This feeling of abandonment was contrary to my theological understanding; nevertheless, it was there. I agonized with God about this for three to four hours, I think.

Then the Word of God began to give me some light. Isaiah 55:5 became a focus. In the 1960s most churches used the King James Version of the Bible, and I did as well.

> Behold, thou shalt call a nation that thou knowest not, and nations that knew not thee shall run unto thee because of the LORD thy God, and for the Holy One of Israel; for he hath glorified thee. Isaiah 55:5 (KJV).

As I meditated on this verse and broke it into sections, I understood God to say, "Behold, thou shalt call **a nation** *that* thou knowest not, **and nations *that* knew not thee shall run unto thee**."

I believed that sentence. A particular nation that I did not know at the time, I would call. Besides that, other nations would run to me. God began to respond to my deep desire with promises of fruitfulness, but not necessarily for the Americans we were working with. Within the next few weeks, while living in Germany, I began to experience something peculiar. On the air base at Bitburg, while I was leading a Bible study with some airmen, a foreign worker at the base, Celso Vidal of Spain, came to serve the table. He could not speak English, and I could not speak Spanish. But he pointed to the Bible we were studying and pointed then to himself.

Through hand gestures, I arranged to meet him again. I found a Puerto Rican airman who was fluent in Spanish to translate for us. He was not a believer but was willing to help us. I shared Christ with Celso, and he responded to the Gospel Bridge illustration that I showed him through the Puerto Rican. He was willing to repent and to ask Jesus to enter his life as his Lord and ruler. We were in the snack bar of the base, and I asked him to pray after me out loud and for the airman to translate my prayer and Celso's prayer in response so that I could be sure that Celso understood. Celso clearly invited Jesus to come into his life, and to run it, and was very pleased with what God was doing for him.

The Puerto Rican was very touched with the presentation of the Gospel and with our prayers. I turned my attention to him, and we talked about the Gospel; he too was eager to accept Christ. So with Celso sitting there, the airman became a new believer too. Later I thought on the significance of leading two Spanish-speaking people from different nations to Christ.

Within a week, a Colombian knocked on our door at the servicemen's center that I ran in Bitburg. His name was Orial. He was looking for work at the air base, and the chaplain had sent him to me to see if I could help. He was fluent in both Spanish and English. He had gone from Colombia to the United States and had found work at Disneyland for a while. Then he had caught a ship to Europe and arrived in France. There he had been robbed of his belongings and his passport. He went to US embassies for help but got none and had finally ended up at the US base and at my doorstep. I was able to help him get a job at the air base as a bagboy at the commissary. In the process, I led him to Christ. In just a couple of weeks after that prayer night, God had brought to me a Spaniard, a Puerto Rican, and a Colombian, three nations, three Spanish speakers. During that same time frame, I went for an overnight stay at a forest inn with two or three men I was discipling. It was near to Luxembourg. There I met a student from Luxembourg who had gone there to be in a quiet place to study for some final exams. As we talked, he came to Christ! God was bringing the nations to me as that verse said. **"And nations *that* knew not thee shall run unto thee."** And he later called us to "**a nation**," Spain, where we labored in the Gospel for seventeen years.

Isaiah 55:5 goes on to say, "Shall run unto thee because of the LORD thy God, and for the Holy One of Israel; for he hath glorified thee."

As you study the Holy One of Israel in the Old Testament, you will discover that the Holy One is Jesus. These people would run to me for Jesus, not for me. They were encountering Jesus through me because God had glorified me in some way. The entire verse came true within only two or three weeks.

But God gave a bonus. During my stay running the servicemen's center, I sent monthly reports to my supervisor in the US Navigator Headquarters, Jim Downing. I still have those reports. In reviewing them this past month, I noticed that after my prayer time, the number of converts to Christ in that ministry was double the normal amount each month until we left in 1966!

God had another surprise in store for me that eventful night. He guided me in the Word to Genesis chapter 32:

> And he said, Thy name shall be called no more Jacob, but Israel: for as a prince hast thou power with God and with men, and hast prevailed. Genesis 32:28 (KJV).

What part of this was for me? God was indicating to me that this was part of His promise to me. "For as a prince hast thou power with God and with men, and hast prevailed." Later I came to understand that God was promising me a special ministry in prayer before His throne, a prevailing ministry. Fifty years later, this book is part of that continuing ministry of prayer. God's promises are not short term. "For the gifts and the calling of God are irrevocable" Romans 11:29.

These promises and predictions to me seemed very great. It seemed that He was offering them and that, for my part, they must be accepted. But they were so significant that I thought that if God did these things, I would risk the danger of pride, a pride that might destroy me. Fear entered my heart. I began to search the Scriptures for a promise of protection from this destruction. I considered the prayer of Jabez:

> Now Jabez called on the God of Israel, saying, "Oh that You would bless me indeed and enlarge my border, and that Your hand might be with me, **and that You would keep *me* from harm that *it* may not pain me**!" And God granted him what he requested. 1 Chronicles 4:10.

I asked God for this promise of protection to go with those promises of blessing that He was offering. I believed He granted my request, so I confirmed with Him that I would accept the entire offer from Him.

If I recall correctly, at that time He guided me to Isaiah 54:

> For a small moment have I forsaken thee; but with great mercies will I gather thee. **In a little wrath I hid my face from thee for a moment; but with everlasting kindness will I have mercy on thee**, saith the LORD thy Redeemer. For this *is as* the waters of Noah unto me: **for *as* I have sworn that the waters of Noah should no more go over the earth; so have I sworn that I would not be wroth with thee, nor rebuke thee.**
>
> For the mountains shall depart, and the hills be removed; **but my kindness shall not depart from thee, neither shall the covenant of my peace be removed**, saith the LORD that hath mercy on thee. Isaiah 54:7–10 (KJV).

This was the final promise of the night (early morning). That sense that God had abandoned me, which did not fit with my theology—God promised that I would never experience that again. I could walk with Him in confidence, safety, and peace. The future would be a good one. The night of prevailing prayer was over, and God had granted me my requests.

As I said earlier, this was my journey. You will have your own. I went to bed, in the early hours of the morning, more than content.

To encourage you to understand that prevailing prayer will help in God's objectives to disciple people, here is the account of an event of life transformation that happened the following year.

One of the servicemen asked me to pray for him. He could never seem to seek God on a regular basis—that is, to have a regular quiet time. He said his heart was cold to the Lord even though he did not want it to be that way.

I put him on my prayer list and prayed for him almost every day. After one year had passed, he was in the same situation and I realized that God was not answering my prayers for him. I got alone with God and with my Bible and asked Him why there was no answer. After some minutes my mind settled on a passage in the book of Judges as Joshua was attempting to conquer the land. "And the LORD was with Judah; and he drave out *the inhabitants of* the mountain; but could not drive out the inhabitants of the valley, because they had chariots of iron" Judges 1:19 (KJV).

I puzzled over this passage. They could not fully take the land because the inhabitants had chariots. But had not God promised them the whole land? Was the problem really the chariots, or was it a lack of faith in God? It came to my mind that the friend I had been praying for was like one of those iron chariots. I was experiencing what the men of Judges were experiencing. They were able to overcome the easy situations but unable to overcome the hard ones. Here was a challenge of faith. I continued in prayer for him more earnestly that afternoon and was looking to God to be able to believe the promises of asking and receiving. As I pressed on in prayer, I seemed to have a block to my faith. I asked God why that was. It was as if He said to me, "You don't really love him, do you, Jack?" Here was something new to consider.

Have you ever experienced that sometimes when you pray for others, God speaks to you about your own life? God was indicating to me to stop looking at the life of my friend but to look at my own life. I realized that I had let a whole year pass without getting serious about my friend's problem.

As I thought about my lack of love for my friend, I asked God to forgive me for my unloving spirit and to fill me with love for my friend. There was no great explosion of love, but I did sense that the Lord was placing love for him in my heart. Galatians 5:6 came to mind, and I began to understand its significance. "For in Christ Jesus neither circumcision nor uncircumcision means anything, but **faith working through love**." My faith was inactive for him because of my lack of love. Love will drive you to believe and to God.

I found that I could now pray for him with faith, that this chariot of iron could be overcome. I got up off of my knees, thanking God that I knew that He would solve my friend's problem according to this: "And all things you ask in prayer, believing, you will receive" Matthew 21:22.

A week later we had a one-week Navigator Discipleship Conference that my friend and I attended. On the fourth day, God touched my friend about the issue of pride. He responded to God and humbled himself. The coldness toward God was removed, and from that time on, he enjoyed a life of walking with God. God had prevailed with him.

What are you facing in your own life or that of another that seems to be a chariot of iron? Seek God for a solution. Set aside some extended time with God to seriously address the issue. Listen to God and see what He has to say about it and what promise He might guide you to.

9

Communion with Christ

The subject of this book is being a change agent for God. This does imply that we are at one with Him and that we are drawing close to His heart, mind, desires, and motives. God invites humans into His inner sanctum. He desires us to know His heart. Walking with God is being with Him, listening to His heart, and Him listening to our hearts.

As we draw near to the Presence of God, the first counsel of the book of James is, "Cleanse your hands, you sinners; and purify your hearts, you double-minded."

He talks about our hands and our hearts. As we approach the Lord, purity is important. Who of us is without sin? We do not want to be obsessed with the idea of sin, but we do want to have our hands cleansed.

> But if we walk in the Light as He Himself is in the Light, we have fellowship with one another, and the blood of Jesus His Son cleanses us from all sin. If we say that we have no sin, we are deceiving ourselves and the truth is not in us. If we confess our sins, He is faithful and righteous to forgive us our sins and to cleanse us from all unrighteousness. 1 John 1:7–9.

His Presence is filled with light. Everything is revealed before Him. Self-deceit cannot be hidden. That is a wonderful thing. What is revealed can be cleansed. Along with the revelation of our imperfections and sin is the accompanying truth that purity of hands is just a confession away. He reminds us that the blood of His Son, Jesus, is the purifying agent. As we come into His Presence, we can wash our hands in the blood of Jesus by asking Him to forgive us.

These verses states that God thinks that the only right thing to do with our sins is to forgive them because the sacrifice of the Lamb was completely sufficient. Cleansing is offered to all who have placed their faith in the Son of God and to all who ask for forgiveness in His name.

God does not forgive us because we deserve it but because the price has already been paid by God Himself on the cross.

During a period of time, I lived in a nation where on the week of remembering the death of Christ, people would afflict themselves by whips and belts of nails fastened to their waists to prove to God that they were worthy. They thought that *their* suffering made them worthy. The Bible says:

> Surely our griefs He Himself bore, and our sorrows He carried; Yet we ourselves esteemed Him stricken, Smitten of God, and afflicted. But He was pierced through for our transgressions, He was crushed for our iniquities; the chastening for our well-being *fell* upon Him, **And by His scourging we are healed**.
> Isaiah 53:4–5.

Jesus went through it all for us. We receive his forgiveness by faith in Him, not by our own suffering.

He promises not only to forgive what we confess, but also to "cleanse us from all unrighteousness." He cleanses us of everything that we have not thought of. The purification is total and complete. We can now stand before Him clean and enjoy the fellowship of the purified.

James warns us about being double-minded, about saying "yes and no." You do have to make up your mind. Do you get forgiveness entirely by the price Jesus paid or partially by your own suffering? You cannot embrace both ideas. Give up your idea of self-suffering and embrace the complete work of Jesus.

James exhorted us to draw near to God with cleansed hands and heart. As we draw near to God in this way, James says God draws near to us. He does this in spirit, and it is real. But I find that as I open the Bible and seek to experience Him through the Word of God, He reveals Himself in a very concrete way. He makes the written Word come alive and personal to me.

Every day my goal is to come before Him, asking Him to purify me and to reveal Himself, His ideas, His heart, and His thoughts through His Word.

The Lord has taught us that our relationship to Him as sons and daughters is permanent. That also means that the term "Father" is permanent. The earthly illustration is the family. Being conceived and being born into a family is irreversible. Your DNA is established forever into your being. But in relating to God and to your earthly family, there is another issue: friendship.

Fatherhood is permanently established, but friendship is dependent on how you and the Father relate to each other.

James brings up this subject by pointing out that Abraham was called the friend of God. He draws this from God's statement in Isaiah 41:8: "But you, Israel, My servant, Jacob whom I have chosen, descendant of **Abraham My friend**..."

To me this carries special significance, as it is God's evaluation of how He related to Abraham. Friendship is not one-sided. Friends *share* intimate feelings and ideas. Joann and I loved each other even though we had not dated very much before marriage. As a result, there were a lot of things that we did not know about each other when we got married. We found that our friendship developed to a much deeper level as we shared life together.

Jesus, at the Last Supper, said:

> You are My friends if you do what I command you. No longer do I call you slaves, for the slave does not know what his master is doing; but I have called you friends, for all things that I have heard from My Father I have made known to you. John 15:14–15.

Here, Jesus states that friends share their intimate thoughts. He shared with them what He was doing and why. Genesis chapter 18 is a very revealing chapter about God thinking of Abraham as a friend. The Lord does a very unusual thing. He and two angels appear as if they were three men walking in the countryside and approach Abraham. He wants to have a meal with Abraham.

Does this remind you of something about Jesus? "Behold, I stand at the door and knock; if anyone hears My voice and opens the door, **I will come in to him and will dine with him, and he with Me**." Revelation 3:20. Do you dine with him, share intimacy with him?

In the Lord's encounter with Abraham, He tells Abraham that about this same time next year, Sarah will give birth to a son. He wants to let him in on this intimate information. The Lord had similarly spoken to me while I was in Norway in 1969, telling me that we would have a child the next year. Why did he tell me that ahead of time? To me, I see this as intimacy from God, doing for me the same as He did for Abraham.

But to return to this encounter with Abraham, God not only told him about the soon-to-be son but also said to the two accompanying angels in Abraham's hearing, "Shall I hide from Abraham what I am about to do?" Genesis 18:17–18. So the Lord tells him that He might have to destroy Sodom and Gomorrah. Abraham knows it is the Lord, but friendship allows dialogue and a differing opinion. A dialogue with God is really prayer. Abraham asks the Lord not to destroy these cities if fifty righteous men are found there. He knows he is bargaining with the LORD (Yahweh in Hebrew) because he calls Him "the Judge of all the earth."

Friendship allows some very bold conversation. Abraham seems to be aware that the lives of hundreds of thousands of people are at stake. He keeps reasoning with the Lord. After asking God to spare the cities if there are fifty righteous, he apparently begins to question his own evaluation of how many righteous may be in those cities, and he reduces the number to forty-five. The Lord says okay, he will spare the cities if there are forty-five.

Oh, that we had many men and women as audacious as Abraham in standing before the throne of God in prayer! Abraham changes the number to forty, then to thirty, then to twenty, and then stops at ten righteous. Abraham understands that his friend, God, has no pleasure in the death of the wicked and even much less in the death of the righteous. The Lord agrees to this request.

The writer of Hebrews encourages us to use the same boldness. "Therefore let us approach the throne of grace **with boldness**, so that we may receive mercy and find grace to help us at the proper time." Hebrews 4:16 (HCSB).

Spiritual boldness is not the boldness of natural humans. It is linked to purity. Coming boldly to the throne is not just deciding to march right in. It includes a respect for the magnificence of God and His holiness. As Abraham talks with God, he demonstrates a very respectful attitude as he changes each number. "Now behold, I have ventured to speak to the Lord, although I am *but* dust and ashes." Genesis 18:27.

Spiritual boldness is linked to a pure heart. Solomon said, "The wicked flee when no one is pursuing, but the righteous are bold as a lion." Proverbs 28:1.

I would offer just a word of caution to this generation, who often link intimacy and disrespect together. Intimacy with God does not imply a disrespectful attitude. True friendship seems to imply a respect for our friend. We don't treat a friend like dirt.

On the subject of communion with Christ, I feel somewhat handicapped. I am an introvert. Communion with Christ includes extroverts. I like a quiet and pensive atmosphere. But you might prefer a noisy one. I do love the song "Shout to the Lord." Shouting, singing out loud, and public displays of emotion are wonderfully worshipful in the proper setting. You may recall King David dancing in the street to the Lord. Shouting can be great worship. **But listening is best in silence.**

Listening prayer. The term seems a contradiction. Prayer is often a two-way street, a conversation. Listening prayer is letting God do His part of the talking. It is being alert to what He wants to say to us. How does He speak to people? He has used many different ways in the past and surely will come up with new ways in the future. We cannot predict how He will speak to us. God's ingenuity is limitless. One example is through what He has made:

> The heavens are telling of the glory of God; and their expanse is declaring the work of His hands. Day to day pours forth speech, and night to night reveals knowledge. There is no speech, nor are there words; their voice is not heard. Their line has gone out through all the earth and their utterances to the end of the world. Psalm 19:1–4.

Hebrews chapter 1 says that God spoke through the prophets to the fathers, but in these last days has spoken to us through the Son. So the Old Testament prophets are part of His voice to us. Don't neglect them. But the most recent word from God comes through His Son, so focus on the New Testament and the teachings of Jesus. Then all the writings after the Gospels are inspired of God, too, as witnessed in 2 Timothy 3:16: "All Scripture is inspired by God and profitable for teaching, for reproof, for correction, for training in righteousness."

Personally, my most normal way to listen to God is with an open Bible before me. But because God enjoys many ways of speaking to us, He is willing to use other methods, too, such as dreams, visions, and so on, as he did with the Apostle Paul and Peter and others, including me.

He speaks to us by the Spirit within us. When we invited Jesus to enter our hearts, the Holy Spirit entered at the same time. This is "the Helper" that Jesus promised just before His death. "I will ask the Father, and He will give you another Helper that He **may be with you forever**; *that is* the Spirit of truth." John 14:16–17. This Helper was given to all the new disciples on the day of Pentecost, fifty days after the resurrection, and to subsequent believers. In fact, God said through the Apostle Paul, "But if anyone does not have the Spirit of Christ, he does not belong to Him." Romans 8:9.

The Spirit resident in us is meant to teach us and remind us of the Word of Christ. "But the Helper, the Holy Spirit, whom the Father will send in My name, He will teach you all things, and bring to your remembrance all that I said to you." John 14:26. One of the evidences of the Spirit within us is being led by Him. "For all who are being led by the Spirit of God, these are sons of God." Romans 8:14.

As we set ourselves to listen to the Holy Spirit and to obey Him, God says:

> But when He, the Spirit of truth, comes, He will guide you into all the truth; for He will not speak on His own initiative, but whatever He hears, He will speak; and He will disclose to you what is to come. John 16:13.

God also communicates His messages through circumstances. What a marvelous wide range of means He uses.

One great obstacle to hearing His voice is that many believers do not believe that He speaks to them. They have not learned to hear His voice. I recommend a book by my good friend Rusty Rustenbach, *A Guide for Listening and Inner-Healing Prayer*. If you have a problem hearing God, this book will help you learn how to hear Him.

If you are one of those who has not believed that God speaks to you, the following may help you to hear Him.

Get out a pen and paper (put the book down for a minute to do this; we will wait). Okay, now with the paper in front of you, ask God to speak to you and record on the paper the *very first thought that comes to your mind*. This is usually the voice of God to you. He usually speaks immediately. Have you written down the phrase that God said to you?

I was in one Christian conference where Rusty had the entire room full of people do this. He then asked people to share what they had heard from God at that moment. A number of people raised their hands, saying that the phrase that immediately came to mind was, "I love you." Don't disregard this thought as your imagination. One of the most important things on God's mind for believers is that they should be assured of His love. Regard this thought as very precious. Respond to it in praise and prayer. This is God's voice to you.

Others who believe that God speaks to them and have experienced His voice will find that the phrase from God for them is something that He has been trying to say to them for some time, but they have ignored His voice. He returns to the subject that He has been trying to get your attention about.

One lady who was learning to listen to God told me that she believed that God had told her to write to her sister. They had been estranged for years. This was extremely hard for her, and it took her three weeks to get up the courage to do it. Listening and obeying God is often not easy, but He will help us to do what He has indicated if we will just come to Him asking for this help.

Be willing to quietly listen to the voice of God on a daily basis.

> For thus the Lord GOD, the Holy One of Israel, has said, "In repentance and rest you will be saved, in quietness and trust is your strength." **But you were not willing.** Isaiah 30:15.

Rusty's book is titled *A Guide for Listening and Inner-Healing Prayer.* Concerning the inner healing part, Joann and I were doing a Bible study with a man and his wife not too long ago. They both had some long-standing spiritual and emotional hang-ups. I have found that instead of months of counseling looking for answers, listening prayer can bring an immediate understanding of the problem source.

We asked this couple to bow their heads and ask God what was the occasion of the beginning of this long-term problem. They bowed their heads, and after just thirty seconds, we asked them what had come to mind. Both of them immediately answered that God had brought to mind a specific incident, a different one for both of them, something that had occurred when they were about ten years old! They were able to describe in detail what had happened. Recognizing the source of their problems enabled us to progress toward a solution. God is so willing to speak to us if we draw near to Him and believe that He will speak to us.

I will insert here another personal example of listening to God. One day while in Bitburg, Germany, I was enjoying fellowship with God and asked Him sincerely if there was *anything* that He wanted to speak to me about. Immediately the idea of being baptized came to mind. This surprised me and confused me. I almost said, "God, are you sure?" That was my thought.

I had been baptized in my church when I was twelve years old. I met Christ about seven years later, but I had considered this baptism valid. Evidently God did not. I was now a full-time missionary for the Navigators and working with chaplains at the US air bases. What would people think if I got baptized again? It would appear that I was not really qualified to do what I was doing. I was embarrassed at the thought of a man in my position getting publicly baptized. But I could not escape the conviction that God was asking this of me. How humbling!

The only solution I could think of was to ask one of the chaplains at the military base if he would baptize me. I was not sure that he would. God, what should I do?

A couple of days later, as I was attending the Sunday chapel service, the chaplain did something that he had never done in the two years I had been attending his services. He announced that he would be glad to baptize anyone who desired to be baptized! Wow, God had immediately presented me with an opportunity. After the service I went up to the chaplain and informed him that I wanted to be baptized. He agreed to do it. A new Christian whom we had led to Christ saw me go up and make my intention known for baptism, and he also came up to be baptized. We got baptized together. He is now a missionary training pastors in India.

If you decide to listen to God, be prepared to do what He asks of you. It will be important, or He would not ask it of you. Take courage; He will work with you to help you, just as He did for me.

In listening to God, we find that He often purifies our hearts and our intentions. David prayed, "Search me, O God, and know my heart; try me and know my anxious thoughts; and see if there be any hurtful way in me, and lead me in the everlasting way." Psalm 139:23–24. God will often answer this prayer through some passage of the Bible.

> For the word of God is living and active and sharper than any two-edged sword, and piercing as far as the division of soul and spirit, of both joints and marrow, and able to judge the thoughts **and intentions of the heart**. Hebrews 4:12.

One practical way of listening to God on a daily basis is to read the Bible each day, telling God that you are listening. I do this daily. I don't get a sense every day that He speaks, but I often do. I have continued this pattern for many years because it yields such great results for my life.

Another way that is very helpful to many people is a good daily devotional book, such as *Streams in the Desert.* Another book people around me comment on and deeply appreciate is *Jesus Calling* by Sarah Young. Remember that these are just devotional books and not the Word of God. These writings are very helpful, and we trust that God will speak to you through them. But as Sarah Young says in her introduction on page xiii, "The Bible is the only infallible, inerrant Word of God."

As an intercessor for others on God's behalf, look to Him carefully to enable you to pray what He would have you pray.

10

Defeating Demonic Forces

> Now after this the Lord appointed seventy others, and sent them in pairs ahead of Him to every city and place where He Himself was going to come. Luke 10:1.
>
> The seventy returned with joy, saying, "Lord, even the demons are subject to us in Your name." Luke 10:17.

Up until now I have addressed your personal issues such as unbelief, faith, holiness, and personal communion with God. Now I want to address the issue of outside forces that we do battle with.

Doing battle with them is not a worrisome thing. Jesus had sent seventy disciples out to minister, and they returned, joyfully declaring that demons were subject to them in the name of Jesus. Why were they joyful? I think it might have been because they saw people oppressed by demons, and they had the authority to free them so that they could live life without this spiritual oppression. My wife and I have seen people freed from this oppression, and we too find joy in their newfound freedom from demon oppression.

The Apostle Paul reminds us that our true struggle is not with ourselves or with other human beings. There are powerful spiritual forces at work against us. We have not been left helpless before them. God has promised us that in fact, they cannot stand against us. But we must understand where our authority lies and what Christ has given us to overcome them. Overcoming is not automatic; it is not just by being believers.

THE FIRST STEP IN OVERCOMING THEM IS AWARENESS OF THEM AND THEIR ACTIVITIES.

Through my church and other Christians in my particular circle, I had heard of Satan or the devil. I knew that Satan had tempted Eve shortly after the creation. After this there is very little mention of him in the Bible until the book of Job in chapters 1 and 2. He takes away Job's wealth and his sons and daughters. Then he takes Job's health, but God does not let him take his life. In all of this, Job has no defense against Satan. He just suffers under his hand.

Then in the New Testament, Jesus has a face-to-face encounter with Satan and overcomes his temptations. All these things I knew.

I had heard that Satan uses our fleshly desires to tempt us. "But each one is tempted when he is carried away and enticed by his own lust." James 1:14. I believed that Satan did not tempt me but that he brought along beautiful girls, opportunities to steal, and so on to be used to tempt me—anything that my lust would respond to. My fleshly desires were the means for Satan to attack me. It was all secondhand, as with Job. At that time I was not even aware that Satan or a demon could attack me directly.

Some of you have grown up in different religious circles where active demonology was taught. It is no surprise to you that Satan or a demon can attack you directly. In conservative evangelical circles, I have found that there is very little awareness of this and hence almost no teaching about how to overcome them. I certainly had none. Even in my preparation for becoming a missionary, I had had no teaching on this subject. My wife and I were left to learn on our own for some years. This is not a criticism, just an observation.

The Gospels are full of illustrations of Jesus casting out demons. At the very beginning of the Gospel of Mark, it is recorded that it was a common thing in the ministry of Jesus. There are many illustrations of this in all the Gospels. Here are two accounts of this ministry in just the first chapter of Mark:

> And He healed many who were ill with various diseases, and cast out many demons; and He was not permitting the demons to speak, because they knew who He was. Mark 1:34.

> And He went into their synagogues throughout all Galilee, preaching and casting out the demons. Mark 1:39.

Please note that he was encountering some of these demonized people in their churches (synagogues).

So we have established that releasing people from the power of demons was a regular part of Jesus's ministry. He transmitted this authority to his laborers (Luke chapter 9 to the twelve Apostles and chapter 10 to the seventy disciples). This may give you some peace that releasing people from the power of spiritual forces is no strange thing for us to do in this twenty-first century if we are ministering as Jesus and the disciples did.

The Apostle Paul has affirmed for us that this forms a part of our spiritual ministry. He also includes that we must prepare ourselves for this spiritual battle by putting on the armor of God and grasping our spiritual sword with which to face the enemy before doing battle:

> Put on the full armor of God, so that you will be able to stand firm against the schemes of the devil. For our struggle is not against flesh and blood, but against the rulers, against the powers, against the world forces of this darkness, against the spiritual *forces* of wickedness in the heavenly *places*. Ephesians 6:11–12.

> And take the helmet of salvation, and the sword of the Spirit, which is the word of God. Ephesians 6:17.

I first became aware of demons in 1965 when we were full-time missionaries running a servicemen's center for American military in Bitburg, Germany. We had three encounters there.

The first, if I recall right, was when our son, Danny, was just a little toddler. One night after we were all in bed, I heard him screaming, terrified. I ran into his room where he was in bed in a crib. He was looking at the small bedroom window as if he had seen there what had terrified him. I felt the skin crawling in the back of my neck as I sensed an evil presence in his room. It was my first encounter. It was scary, and I did not know what to do. I had heard somewhere that the Word of God and the blood of Jesus were powerful against the enemy. I declared my faith in the blood of Jesus and began reciting Scripture verses that I had memorized. Soon the sense of an evil presence disappeared, and Danny was no longer terrified and went back to sleep. That was my first warning that evil spirits were around but that we could defeat them.

The second incident occurred to me personally. Everything was going well with our ministry to these servicemen, but a spirit of discouragement fell over me without a cause. It puzzled me. This discouragement continued for about two weeks, and I began to wonder if it was demonic. One night in bed before going to sleep, I—in my mind, not out loud—told a demon to go away and leave me alone if he was there causing this. For the next couple of days, the discouragement continued. My silent prayer had been unsuccessful.

Two nights later, as I was in bed and Joann was asleep, I decided to speak to the demon, if that is what it was, but this time out loud. The time before I had been embarrassed to speak out loud because Joann might hear me and think it was weird. I overcame this fear that I would be embarrassed and said out loud but quietly, "If there is a demon here bothering me, go in Jesus's name." I lay down and went to sleep. For the next week, I was free of this mysterious discouragement. Then it came back again. I had not learned that I could tell a demon to go and to not come back again. So when I realized that it might have returned, I told it out loud again to leave. The discouragement left right away and did not return to me.

I am not trying to say that everybody who gets discouraged is being attacked by a demon. There are many reasons for discouragement. Mine, at that time, was caused by a spiritual force that Paul described in Ephesians 6.

The next awareness was with a US airman at the air base. He recounted to me that one evening he and some others gathered to play with a Ouija board. They put their hands on the board and asked it a question. The object moved, touching alphabet letters to spell out the answer. They thought that it has a harmless, mysterious game.

When the airman went to bed that night in his dorm, he was frightened to see a little demon perched at the foot of his bunk. By playing the game, he had attracted a demon to him. This airman later became one of the men we discipled at that base.

These years in Germany were just the beginning of various encounters with demons. Later I traveled to various countries over the next few years. In each instance demons were overcome with the Name and power of Jesus. New understanding came with each new encounter.

My purpose in recounting these encounters is to convince you that these demons are real and can be overcome. I will end the illustrations of these encounters with one final illustration that occurred twenty-five years after the first ones.

We had returned to the United States and came for a conference to Glen Eyrie, the Navigators' headquarters in Colorado Springs. It was an advanced counseling seminar led by Larry Crabb, a noted counselor. While there we encountered some old friends who had been missionaries in South Korea and were taking the course. Somehow we had gotten on to the subject of demon oppression. One friend described an experience he had had in Korea with a very deep pressure on his chest, as if someone were sitting on him. He attributed it to a demon.

During our conversation, Joann said that she was experiencing a choking sensation while attending the seminar and that it was very distracting to her learning from the sessions. Someone wanting to honor us had lodged us in the Pink House at Glen Eyrie, which had been built by a previous owner, a Texas oil man, who had it built as his private residence there. The strange part was that over thirty years earlier, when Joann was single and employed by the Navigators, she had been housed there. During that time thirty years earlier, she had had the same choking sensation, and a doctor had prescribed some medication to relieve the choking. As we talked with our missionary friends, it occurred to us that this very distracting choking may be caused by a demon. Right then we prayed and commanded the demon to leave if this was caused by him. Immediately Joann was released from the choking sensation.

These have been illustrations of fear, distraction, and depression. There are more serious attacks of demons such as pornography, addictions, fits of anger, and almost any evil thing that could be mentioned.

THE SECOND STEP IS TO REALIZE THAT CHRIST HAS COMPLETE AUTHORITY OVER THEM.

The book of Colossians has as its major theme the greatness of Christ Jesus. Jesus is the creator of all these spiritual forces that we do battle with. He did not create these authorities to be evil. Some of these angelic forces that were meant for good turned to the dark side. Satan was evidently the lead angel who went bad. He created a rebellion in the heavens, and one-third of the angels rebelled with him and were cast out of heaven. These are probably the demons that do battle with us. Satan is especially referred to in two books of the Bible, Isaiah and Ezekiel. In Ezekiel he is referred to as the King of Tyre in chapter 28:

> Thus says the Lord GOD, "**You had the seal of perfection, Full of wisdom and perfect in beauty.** You were in Eden, the garden of God; Every precious stone was your covering: The ruby, the topaz and the diamond; The beryl, the onyx and the jasper; the lapis lazuli, the turquoise and the emerald; and the gold, the workmanship of your settings and sockets, was in you. On the day that you were created they were prepared. You were the anointed cherub who covers, and I

placed you *there*. You were on the holy mountain of God; you walked in the midst of the stones of fire. **You were blameless in your ways from the day you were created until unrighteousness was found in you.**

By the abundance of your trade you were internally filled with violence, and you sinned. Therefore, I have cast you as profane from the mountain of God. And I have destroyed you, O covering cherub, from the midst of the stones of fire. **Your heart was lifted up because of your beauty**; you corrupted your wisdom by reason of your splendor. **I cast you to the ground**; I put you before kings, that they may see you. Ezekiel 28:12–17.

How art thou fallen from heaven, O Lucifer, son of the morning! *how* art thou cut down to the ground, which didst weaken the nations! For thou hast said in thine heart, I will ascend into heaven, **I will exalt my throne above the stars of God**: I will sit also upon the mount of the congregation, in the sides of the north: I will ascend above the heights of the clouds; **I will be like the Most High**. Yet thou shalt be brought down to hell, to the sides of the pit. Isaiah 14:12–15 (KJV).

Satan was created beautiful and wise and was given trusted positions by Christ. He violated this trust and became proud and wanted to dethrone God. He was cast out, along with those who followed him. Satan and his followers are these "principalities, rulers, and powers" that have been cast down to the earth. They are disruptive but defeated.

Jesus defeated Satan in the forty days of testing. He demonstrated his authority over these evil forces day after day while ministering for those three years. One of the reasons that Jesus had in coming to the earth, as the Apostle John said in 1 John 3:8, was "to destroy the works of the devil." The Father has granted Jesus full authority over all spiritual powers. We should rejoice in this, as cited here:

> For by Him [Jesus] all things were created, *both* in the heavens and on earth, visible and invisible, whether thrones or dominions or rulers or authorities—all things have been created through Him and for Him. Colossians 1:16.

> For in Him all the fullness of Deity dwells in bodily form, and in Him you have been made complete, and He is the head over all rule and authority.
> Colossians 2:9–10.

> When He had disarmed the rulers and authorities, He made a public display of them, having triumphed over them through Him. Colossians 2:15.

> *These are* in accordance with the working of the strength of His might which He brought about in Christ, when He raised Him from the dead and seated Him at His right hand in the heavenly *places*, **far above all rule and authority and power and dominion**, and every name that is named, not only in this age but also in the one to come. And He put all things in subjection under His feet, and gave Him as head over all things to the church, which is His body, the fullness of Him who fills all in all. Ephesians 1:19–23.

Jesus has complete authority over the enemy and all of his forces. When Jesus was through letting Satan test Him, He gave him a simple order to go:

> Then Jesus said to him, "Go, Satan! For it is written, 'YOU SHALL WORSHIP the LORD your GOD, AND SERVE HIM ONLY.'" Then the devil left Him; and behold, angels came and *began* to minister to Him. Matthew 4:10–11.

It would help us to realize that Satan is not a close second to Jesus. The Word of God says that Jesus is "**far above all rule and authority and power and**

dominion." There is a huge gap between the power of Jesus and the power of Satan. They are not struggling for supremacy. Jesus has already defeated Satan, and we walk in the assurance of this victory.

Jesus has defeated Satan, but He has not expelled him from the earth. He lives here and exercises his power within the limits that God has decided. He has his own forces, demons, and has given them spiritual positions of power within where he attempts to rule. His purpose is to resist God and to hold sway over other people. In the first century, Satan resided in Turkey.

> And to the angel of the church in Pergamum write: The One who has the sharp two-edged sword says this: "I know where you dwell, where Satan's throne is." Revelation 2:12–13.

So we are well aware of Satan and his activities. The Apostle Paul states that we wrestle with Satan and with his leaders.

> For our struggle is not against flesh and blood, but against the rulers, against the powers, against the world forces of this darkness, against the spiritual *forces* of wickedness in the heavenly *places*. Ephesians 6:12.

Our ministry is to rescue people from Satan's power as Christ has rescued us.

> For He rescued us from the domain of darkness, and transferred us to the kingdom of His beloved Son. Colossians 1:13.

These forces attempt to stop the work of God, but as we walk in Christ, we know that we can victoriously battle these forces. Jesus said, "I will build my church; and all the powers of hell shall not prevail against it." Matthew 16:18 (TLB).

We worked in Spain and Western Europe for many years, and at times I would sense, like a covering cloud over the nation, a cloud of doubt and unbelief that settled over both the believers and unbelievers. I believe that cloud of spiritual darkness can be dispelled by believers of strong faith.

THE THIRD STEP IS TO CONSIDER THAT JESUS DELEGATED THIS AUTHORITY TO US.

Not long after Jesus appointed twelve men to accompany Him, He called them together and gave them authority for the following: "He gave them power and authority to drive out all demons." Luke 9:1 (NIV). This was not something they learned through experience. It was given to them by Jesus, who has all authority. This was power and authority over *all* demons. This is an astounding authority and power. No demons could stand before them. There was recorded one exception, and we will go over this later.

Then in Luke 10, Jesus calls seventy other disciples to Him and gives them this same authority, sending them out two by two to preach and minister. I don't think I fall into the category of the twelve special apostles, but I do think that I (and any believer who is serving God) fall into the category of the seventy. When He sends them out, it does not record that He specifically gave them this authority over demons, but as they return from their mission, they declare that this had been true for them.

> The seventy returned with joy, saying, "Lord, even the demons are subject to us in Your name." And He said to them, "I was watching Satan fall from heaven like lightning. Behold, I have given you authority to tread on serpents and scorpions, and over all the power of the enemy, and nothing will injure you."
> Luke 10:17–19.

This is a very important passage. Let us try to understand it well, for someday you may need to cast out a demon for yourself or for another.

Just as Jesus encountered demons as He ministered, so did the seventy. In their own words, they found that "the demons are subject to us in Your name." "Subject to them" means that the demons had to do whatever the disciples told them to do; they were *subject* to the disciples.

The next important point was that the disciples' authority rested in Jesus's name. Who they were was unimportant. It was who Jesus is. Our authority and power is in Christ, not in ourselves. Whenever we command the demons to do something, such as leave, we need to do it in the name of Jesus.

Jesus then informs the disciples that He was present when Satan was cast out of heaven, rapidly, like a lightning bolt. He then reminds them of the authority that He Himself had given them: "Behold, I have given you authority to tread on serpents and scorpions, and over all the power of the enemy, and nothing will injure you."

As demons are dangerous, Jesus lets the disciples know that they will have the demons under their feet but that they do not need to fear them, for the demons are forbidden to harm them. He clearly said, "And over all the power of the enemy." Whatever the power of the enemy, the seventy have more.

The seventy had authority over demons. If you have authority, you can command. We normally obey police officers, not for how powerful they are but because they have been given authority over us by some higher authority. The same principle is in effect between demons and us disciples. When we are facing them, we should command them in the name of Jesus to go and to not return.

I have noticed that most people believe they should pray to God to have the demons leave. Jesus's pattern of dealing with demons in the Gospels was to talk to them and to give them direct commands. When facing a demon, Jesus did not go off and pray and ask God to handle them. Jesus had the authority to command them. We have this same authority. Rather than praying to God to tell them to go, we should use our God-given authority and give them commands out loud.

It is very much like the Gospel. If someone needs to hear the Gospel, we are commanded to share it with him or her. We don't pray and ask God to share the Gospel with that person. He has given us authority and responsibility to tell everyone the good message. So with demons, we should address them directly, as we have been given authority to do this. Don't ask God to do what God has asked you to do.

That does not mean that we should not prepare ourselves in prayer if we are going into battle with them; we should. And we should be in a spirit of prayer as we address them and overcome them. We should take some time beforehand to cleanse our lives and rededicate ourselves to His Lordship.

We must learn to recognize demonic activity.

In the first page of this chapter, I said we need to be aware of demons' influence. Now I want to address how to recognize their activity. Many times they are active in people's lives, but we may attribute what they are doing to a normal human activity. If someone is acting strangely, we may see his or her actions as stress, fear, or some other normal human experience.

In trying to understand and recognize demonic activity, we must not make the mistake of seeing everything as demonic. Some people see demons under every bush and rock and so become preoccupied with them. Others are oblivious to them and never see a demon under any rock or bush. Both extremes are a mistake. Don't attribute everything to them, and don't attribute nothing to them. Learn to identify their activities.

These forces are normally defeated by using our God-given authority over them and commanding them to leave, just as Jesus, the twelve apostles, and the seventy disciples did. Prayer is applied to things that God must do. Obedience and the use of our authority is applied to what we must do. As I said earlier, God has told us to share the Gospel with the world. Don't pray and ask God to share the Gospel with our friends; He asks us to do this. In the same way, He asks us to command demons to leave.

As this is a book about prayer, I won't go into more detail on the subject of demons. I have written a booklet titled *Overcoming Spiritual Forces of Evil.* You can get it by contacting me at jackblanch@mindspring.com.

11

Praying for Those outside of the Kingdom of God

We know how God views the unsaved world. Redemption is at the heart of God. He has no pleasure in judgment; His pleasure is in redeeming people. He desires all people to be saved.

We know that he has enlisted all believers in the task of bringing people to redemption. The intercessor understands the heart of God for the world and prays accordingly. The Trinity is groaning over humankind, and God's desire is to bring humankind to repentance. Love is the reason for this groaning. When we pray for the unsaved, the heart of God leaps for joy.

Mortality Meets Immortality
How will this heavenly Being
who dwells in unapproachable light
whose holiness burns like a fire
whose dwelling is immortality
reveal His love to the mortal and unholy
without destroying the beloved object?

His messenger will be human
A redeemed mortal, a godlike man or woman

One who can embrace mortality and unholiness
With his Maker's eternal love and compassion
To bring peace and reconciliation
To the one who stretches out his or her hand to the Immortal
For eternal healing to his or her soul

—Jack Blanch

Just as Jesus is the mediator between God and humans, so the intercessor can be a mediator between humans and God. His or her task is to be God's representative before the throne of Christ.

When I say "God's representative," I mean praying with the love and compassion that God has. God listens not to the mouth of the believer but to his or her heart.

There is such a thing as a closed heart toward another or an indifferent heart when we are praying. How do you think God would respond to the closed or indifferent heart?

Evaluate for a moment how you pray for people like those in the list that the Apostle Paul mentions: "immorality, impurity, sensuality, idolatry, sorcery, enmities, strife, jealousy, outbursts of anger, disputes, dissensions, factions, envying, drunkenness, carousing, and things like these." Can you intercede for these people with fervent love?

When a person's heart turns to the Lord, it is a great occasion for rejoicing. Not only does that person receive eternal life, but also he or she gets cleansed from all of his or her sins. He or she is forgiven for murder, rape, thievery, lying, and so on. So while praying for someone to come to Christ, we can pray with joy and happiness for the wonderful cleansing that that person will receive.

> But God demonstrates His own love toward us, in that while we were yet sinners, Christ died for us. Romans 5:8.

> For God so loved the world, that He gave His only begotten Son, that whoever believes in Him shall not perish, but have eternal life. For

> God did not send the Son into the world to judge the world, but that the world might be saved through Him. John 3:16–17.

Redemption is at the heart of God. He has no pleasure in judgment; His pleasure is in redeeming people:

> God was in Christ reconciling the world to Himself, not counting their trespasses against them, and He has committed to us the word of reconciliation. Therefore, we are ambassadors for Christ, as though God were making an appeal through us; we beg you on behalf of Christ, be reconciled to God. 2 Corinthians 5:19–20.

The intercessor understands the heart of God for the world and prays accordingly, confident that, "The Lord is not wishing for any to perish but for all to come to repentance." 2 Peter 3:9.

How do we pray for the lost?

Who are the people you are praying for? We normally do not pray for people in general. We pray for a nation, a city, relatives, friends, enemies, and so on. We usually know something about this person or people group. I usually pray according to what I know about them.

Here are some examples:

- Nations or people who have had a form of Christianity without power or new life:

  "God, would you bring someone their way who is living the transformed life, someone who would answer them in a clear way so that they can understand Your reality?"
- Nations or people who are atheists:

  "God, bring them an awareness of Your presence and power. Make them discontent with a life without long-term meaning or purpose so that they might search for meaning and for You."
- People who have been hurt or offended by Christians or churches:

  "Lord, would you bring to them a believer of compassion and understanding to enable them to see that You were not the one hurting them and see that you have paid a great price to reconcile them and are seeking them?"

- People who don't like God and what He does:

  "Lord, let them meet a messenger of Yours who has a deep love for them and does good to them in the name of Christ, representing You and Your feelings."
- People who have had no teaching about God or of the Christian way and have not sought Him:

  "Lord, stir up their spirits to sense a need for You. Bring a believer their way who will approach them in a spirit of love and compassion and create a hunger for knowing and finding You."
- For your friends, relatives, or acquaintances who need Christ:

  "Christ, stir up my love and heart to reach out to them. Convince me of my negligence and lack of love for them and my lack of obedience to Christ to win them to Him."

How do we pray for the intercessor—you?

What do intercessors need? They need an non-hypocritical heart toward our acquaintances. King David said, "If *I* regard wickedness in *my* heart, The Lord will not hear." Psalm 66:18.

They need a heart of compassion. We often are very unsympathetic toward immoral people we know.

They need a Christlike spirit. He came to seek and to save the lost sheep.

They need a heart of faith. As we pray the promises, we need the help of His Spirit to believe, to pray with confidence.

> If we ask anything according to His will, we know that He hears us, and if we know that He hears us, we know that we have the petitions we asked for. 1 John 5:14,15.

> For the eyes of the Lord are toward the righteous, and His ears attend to their prayers. 1 Peter 3:12.

One year, when my family and I were on furlough from our mission assignment, we regularly attended a very wonderful church in Oregon. It was a growing church. In the year we attended it, membership was regularly on the rise. And our family was blessed by its ministry to us.

On our last Sunday there before returning to Spain, the pastor invited me up to the platform and asked me to share any word I desired with the congregation. This was a special honor, as I had never seen him do this before.

There had been one thing about the church that I thought would be helpful for them. There were eight hundred to one thousand in the audience. I asked everyone who had come to Christ through the ministry for this church, apart from the children's program, to please raise his or her hand.

As we looked around this large gathering, only three or four people raised their hands. I then sat down. At the end of the service, one of the lead elders approached me and said it was a powerful revelation to him about the need of their church.

Someone shared with me recently about a Barna Church Survey that recorded that 95 percent of church members had never led anyone to Christ.

Are you one of those 95 percent?

I believe that almost everyone reading this book on prayer could become part of the 5 percent. I believe the steps to solving this are simple.

1. Believe that God has appointed you (as with all believers) to be an ambassador of Christ to deliver the message of the Gospel.
2. Abide in Christ so that the love of Christ motivates you to reach people for His sake.
3. Pray and ask the Father to give you the privilege to personally lead another to Christ.
4. If you believe He will answer, prepare yourself with a simple Gospel presentation so that you can lead a seeker to Christ.
5. Be alert for God to bring someone your way who has a prepared heart.

Don't be afraid; God will help you.

Here are some examples of God bringing prepared hearts to someone who is following the above five steps.

When I was about twenty, I was attending Navigator Bible studies. I became desirous to bring others to Christ and was praying for this. I asked one of the mature men in the group to teach me how to present the Gospel. He showed me the Bridge to Life illustration by the Navigators, which illustrates that Jesus is the bridge to God.

With a believing friend, I practiced presenting this illustration to a hungry person.

One day as I was drawing out this illustration on a piece of paper, I found out that I was that hungry person. I asked myself when I had made this step across the Bridge to eternal life. I could not answer the question. After about two weeks of wrestling through this question I decided to go home and ask Jesus into my life in case He was outside (I didn't know and was confused).

I was sure that if Jesus came into my life, He would want to run it, to be my Lord and ruler. After some struggle, I did invite Him to come into my life as Lord.

I became my first convert.

Often, I would ask God to enable me as a new believer to lead others to Christ. As I pray, God brings people to me, although I am willing to go to them.

A couple of years ago, a young man attended a Bible study that I attended at the YMCA. After some Bible discussion, it became evident to me that he did not know Christ. After the study, I invited him to breakfast at McDonald's. I took a napkin and slowly drew out the Bridge to Life illustration. I asked him if he had ever crossed the Bridge from death to life. To my surprise, he said yes.

Because just thirty minutes before, he had shown no evidence of Christ in his life, I asked him when he had crossed the Bridge. His answer was that while I was drawing the illustration, he had done that. He added that while I was drawing it, he had the sensation that Jesus was sitting on the bench alongside of him.

Just a few days ago, I had a similar experience. I was explaining the Bridge and eternal assurance to a believer who knew someone who had a hang-up. This person was taking each of the steps to God as I explained then to make sure she was on the right side. She did not take them out loud, but afterward she told me she had been following right long and taking the steps as I talked.

In chapter 8, "Prevailing Prayer," I recounted how after praying for God to bless me in evangelism, He gave me a promise that He would bring people to me. I recounted how over the next couple of weeks, He brought three people to me who came to Christ. He does delight in answering prayer and in bringing people to Himself.

In Germany I led another airman to Christ at the US base. About a week after leading him to Christ, I was concerned that if he met a person who was prepared in his or her heart to meet God, would he know what to do? I met with him and showed him this verse: "For the wages of sin is death, but the free gift of God is eternal life in Christ Jesus our Lord." Romans 6:23. I pointed out to him that all the elements of the Gospel were in that one verse. As he was a new Christian, he did not know much about the Bible, so I encouraged him to memorize that verse in case he met a prepared person.

A week later, we met again, and he recounted how in the barracks hall at the drinking fountain, he met another airman. The airman was totally prepared in heart to meet God, and so was the new believer with his one verse. He led that airman to Christ right there in the hall! The new believer was only two weeks old in Christ.

We need to be convinced that many people are prepared of God and to be looking for them.

In Spain we dealt with many college students who were atheists. We learned that if we could get a person into a Gospel of John discussion for about three months, over 90 percent of them came to Christ. I trained new converts in this method and encouraged them not to push for decisions right away.

One of the men who joined a study group was a believer in God but not converted. He told me later that he would have received Christ the first week but that they made him wait three months before encouraging him to receive Christ. I learned from that.

Getting others to pray adds power to the prayers for unbelievers (or anyone else, for that matter).

As an example of this, there was a secular Jew attending the Bible study I attended. After attending the Bible study for about two years, I became deeply burdened for this man. He had been coming to the Bible study for fourteen years without meeting Christ. This speaks a lot for the study group that it could keep a person like him coming back. One day one of the group members asked him (in a friendly way) why he kept coming. He answered that he always felt better for being there.

I was deeply burdened because it appeared that after fourteen years, he was no closer to coming to Christ than at the beginning. I thought, if we don't do something soon, this eighty-year-old man is going to die without Christ.

I have a large group of prayers on an e-mail list. They are my resource for praying for all of our needs and ministry. I sent out an emergency prayer note, telling them about this man and asking them to join me in urgent prayer for my friend and colleague in Bible study. They began praying immediately.

About three weeks later, at Bible study one morning when he and I were alone, I asked this man a personal question about his life just to get to know him better (he was always silent in the Bible study), and he responded by putting his head in his hands and commenting, "What a great sinner I am." Wow, what a reaction. I said no more, observing the God was at work in him.

After approximately another three weeks, it was Easter season. While he was watching a movie on the crucifixion, upon the scene of the Roman soldier piercing the side of Jesus with a sword, this man felt the pain of the sword entering his own side and at that moment made his identification with Christ as his savior!

God did the unexpected in drawing that man to Himself. He is now a very precious believer and a great example to every one of the love of Christ. He has been a believer for about two years now.

Sometimes God takes more than six weeks to answer our prayers. When I was drafted during the Korean War, I entered the submarine service. I had been a submarine reservist for about two years prior to that. When I joined the crew of my new submarine, I began to pray for the crew. I was the only believer among the 110 men aboard.

I had the opportunity to share Christ on various occasions. One person, the cook, had a lot of questions because he had Mormons visiting him every week he was not out to sea. They confused him a lot, and I was not very up on their doctrines since I had only known Christ for about two years.

One day, after being aboard about two months, as I was on deck watch while going through the Panama Canal, the chef came topside for some fresh air where I was standing watch. He asked me about baptism, which was very important to Mormons. I did not know much about it, but as I started to talk on the subject, a strange thing happened to me. I had some kind of brain disconnect and could not understand what I was saying to him about baptism. This continued for three to four minutes as I recall, and then my brain reconnected to what I was saying, which was "Do you understand it?" He said yes and went back down the hatch. I was left there, wishing I could have understood the explanation, thinking it was God's answer to him. He came to Christ about three months later.

The next incident aboard ship came about six months after that. I was now in charge of the torpedo room and had three young seamen as helpers. We were lifting a two-thousand-pound torpedo for maintenance. One of us was at each of the four corners, manning block and tackle so that it did not fall. You don't want a live torpedo falling inside a submarine.

As we worked, the three started asking questions about God. They were very open. During the maintenance time, all three of them accepted Christ. God was still answering my prayers for the crew.

It is not unusual for God to create unusual circumstances to bring an encounter about if you are praying for God to bring to you prepared people. When I got discharged from the navy, I stayed with my brother for a few days. One day I needed to go from San Jose to Oakland about employment. He loaned me his car, and I headed out. I knew San Jose very well, but to my surprise, I got lost getting out of town. I stopped at a stop sign, and as I stopped, one of the tires went flat. Very strange. I looked in the trunk, and the spare tire was flat. I looked, and there was no jack. It took me most of the day to solve the problem, and I returned home without accomplishing my objective.

The following day I started out for Oakland again. About twenty minutes into the trip, I picked up a teenage hitchhiker who was going to a job interview in the direction I was going. In those days, it was legal to hitchhike. As we drove along, I mentioned something about God. He said, "I am searching for God." I began to share the Gospel, and I glanced over at him as I was driving. His jaw was literally hanging open in amazement as he listened to the Gospel. When we stopped at the place where he hoped to get employment, he received Christ joyfully.

Well, I waited for him to have his interview, and as he had no transportation, I took him back home. It was lunchtime, and as we entered his house, his mother was preparing lunch and invited me to join them, as I had befriended her son. During lunch the subject of his conversion came up, and she also was very prepared and desirous to know God. She did not make a decision at that time. The next day I started again for Oakland. God will interrupt your plans for an eternal event.

Are you prepared with a gospel presentation?

- One effective presentation that I have used often is the Bridge to Life illustration, which you can get online from the Navigators at http://www.navigators.org/Tools/Evangelism.
- Here is another simple one for someone who believes that Jesus is the Son of God and that He rose from the dead. Many people who have attended church, though often unconverted, hold these beliefs:

> That if you confess with your mouth Jesus *as* Lord, and believe in your heart that God raised Him from the dead, you will be saved; for with the heart a person believes, resulting in righteousness, and with the mouth he confesses, resulting in salvation…for whoever will call on the name of the Lord will be saved. Romans 10:9, 10, and 13.

Here are a few ideas:

1. "Confess Jesus as Lord." The Lord is the ruler of all, which should include your life.
2. "Believe in your heart that God raised Him from the dead." Truly believe that He rose from the dead.
3. "With the mouth he confesses, resulting in salvation…for whoever will call on the name of the Lord will be saved." Calling on the name of Jesus will save you if you believe the first two points.
   - A third way I use to present the Gospel is for people who doubt there is a God, or who doubt that Jesus is the Son of God.

I am the author of *What If God Exists?* This book was written for atheists and agnostics. As they are reading, if they are convinced by what they read about God and Jesus, I offer the prayer for salvation on page 125:

> Father God, I am in agreement with you that my deeds and ways of living have been wrong and I ask your forgiveness. I have come to believe that you Jesus, are the Son of God, and I invite you to enter my life. I have every intention of following you, but please give me the strength necessary to do it. Thank you for coming into my life in response to this prayer and for giving me eternal life.

What If God Exists? by Jack Blanch can be obtained at amazon.com in either paperback or as an eBook.

Here is my prayer for the unsaved: "Lord, I pray that You would draw people to You, something that I have no power to do. I know that You long to bring them to redemption. Jesus, You paid the price for all their sins, and it must touch You deeply that Your payment goes unclaimed for so many people in the world. Realize the desire of Your heart by 'bringing many sons into glory.' When You do this, incline my heart to give You all of the praise for this great work. May I claim nothing for myself. How terrible it would be to claim the work of God as my work. Be praised in everything, dear Lord. Amen."

12

Expanding Your Prayer Horizons

"Be still, and know that I *am* God."
Psalm 46:10 (KJV).

With the following comments, I don't mean to imply that in a crowded atmosphere or in a short quiet time, you cannot hear the voice of God. You can. But I want to stir up an additional option.

There is something special about being quiet before God. The troubled and occupied mind is filled with background noise. It drowns out the voice of God. It distracts us, confuses us, and leaves almost no space for the holy voice of God.

Do you want to hear the voice of God? Have you ever heard two channels playing at once? Neither channel comes out clearly. Are you asking God to please speak up and to make a clear sound over the noise that fills your mind and ears? Do you deny God his request to "Be still, and know that I *am* God"? Do you say to God that you don't want to just be still, you want Him to speak up louder? You want to set the terms.

How would you create a still, quiet space in your mind or life? Your workday does not allow for this. You must be at a certain place at an appointed time. You must give those work hours your undivided attention, for the most part. To attempt to hear the voice of God while you are working is probably a bad idea. You would not be honoring your commitment to your employer, if you have one.

Then, when you return home after a long or short commute, rest, food, or responsibilities are next on the agenda. Kids, a spouse, a roommate, a pet are all demanding attention; even the house or apartment makes its own demands. Day after day the cycle repeats itself, and days turn into months and years. The voice of God is still waiting to catch your attention. Oh, you attend church, sing, listen to sermons, converse with friends. But the Friend quietly waits without a protest, apparently.

Is God ever disappointed? Does He long for quiet talks, and does He retreat when He is ignored? Could God be that sensitive? Isaiah says, "Truly, You are a God who hides Himself, O God of Israel, Savior!" Isaiah 45:15.

What does Isaiah mean, a God who hides Himself? It seems that He reveals Himself to the honest seeker. It pleases God to hide His wisdom from the proud and the wise in their own eyes.

Do you remember the experience of Elijah the prophet? He traveled forty days and forty nights to get to the mountain of God and to hear His voice. He was in a cave and heard a mighty wind that was breaking the rocks upon the mountain, but God was not in that. Next came an earthquake, but God was not in that. Then came a great fire, but God was not in that. Lastly, there came a quiet breeze where he heard the voice of God. Can you get to a quiet place in your heart and your surroundings?

Prayer and Fasting Times: Friday Noon to Sunday Noon

Twenty-eight years ago, Joann and I felt a need to hear God more clearly, so we decided to take a weekend to fast and pray. It was with some trepidation because we had never fasted before. We took some fruit juice with us and rented a motel in a quiet place where we could get out and walk if we wanted. Having no meals meant we had no schedule and could let the nights and days run together as we wished. We had some time together in the Word and prayer, but it was mostly both of us alone seeking to hear the Lord. To our surprise, because we were not thinking of food, we did not get hungry. We only had a light breakfast the morning of our departure on Sunday to give us strength to drive home and some fruit juice on occasion during the weekend.

We spent time in worship and with the open Bible, listening to God. The times with God were very precious. We felt cleansed spiritually and in tune with God. This worked so well that we later established this as a pattern for ourselves. We began to have these getaways one to three times a year. If your health permits, we encourage you to do this. In our mideighties, we find we can no longer do this. Try it while you are still young enough. Your life will be enriched.

Five-Day Retreats to Listen to God and to Pray

We have done this at least five different times in four different nations in Africa, Spain, and South America. The result of each was unique. Usually the purpose was to deepen the spiritual lives of the participants or to further the work of God in that particular nation.

We would usually make an agreement with the mission workers of that nation to clear their schedules of all responsibilities for five days. We would get a retreat center or a home where we could pray. Our schedule was to pray from 8:00 a.m. to 12:00 p.m., have a meal break for one hour, and then to pray again from 1:00 p.m. to 5:00 p.m.—eight hours daily. The evenings were free. We were not fasting, just praying. The following is an evaluation of each of these retreats.

Buenos Aires, Argentina

Rusty Rustenbach and I led this time. Lee Brase of the US Navigators gave us good direction. There were about eight to ten of us praying, mostly missionaries.

We asked everybody to put aside agendas and just wait on God. This is difficult because most mission leaders have an agenda that they want to accomplish. But our purpose was only to listen to what God has to say.

In this case, Rusty and I were invited because the missionaries had issues that were not being resolved.

I remember that after only two hours of prayer and worship on the first day, one of the missionaries said, "Enough of this. We have issues that we need to solve." How hard it is to believe that listening to God solves things. Rusty and I directed them to continue listening to God and to not enter into discussion of their problems. We did that.

During those five days, we had some marvelous time of Bible reading, praise, worship, and hymn singing. We did this in a conference center that had a large auditorium and other smaller rooms. As there were only ten of us, we had a small room while another large Christian group had the auditorium. On the second day, the director of the large group asked us to please leave our door open when we were singing, even though they were meeting. God blessed our singing so much that, even without any musical instruments, I would describe our singing as angelic. God was blessing us and the other conference.

As we looked at God in the Scriptures and listened to Him day after day, our hearts were transformed. By the fourth day, Rusty and I felt at liberty to open the time up for the missionaries to discuss their issues.

To the surprise of all of us, the time of looking at God and listening to Him had given all a different perspective on their disagreements and problems. *Not one person had an unresolved issue to discuss!* Getting God's perspective changed their perspective on the problems. Everything that they had seen as a problem before was now seen as a blessing from God!

Because we had spent so much time together worshiping (eight hours a day), we had great freedom of expression, lifting our arms while praying, and so on. At one point one of us, as his arms were raised in praise, felt power going out through his arms, out the window, and toward the city and people who were on his heart. How special. Healing and power were present.

One of the university ministries in Argentina had come to a stop that year. The week after this prayer and listening time, one of the persons counseled the one in charge of this ministry to stop trying to make things happen and to instead go to the university, sit and have coffee outside, and just pray for the next two weeks. Within just a couple of hours, a student came out, recognized him, and sat down. Later that day, other students came and sat. The ministry was restarted. Isn't God wonderful?

In that same city, we discovered that a missionary's wife had not told anyone before that at night she would see a fearsome, demonic face looking through her bedroom window. We used our authority in Christ and told the demon to leave. As far as I know, she never had that problem again.

One of the missionaries arranged interviews for me with two Argentine intercessors. This has been a highlight of my life as I recall what they shared (I taped one of the interviews).

One of them recounted the results of visiting a pastor's son at the pastor's home. The pastor had a grown son whom he never brought to church and kept pretty much in the house. The intercessor went to the pastor's home to deliver a church paper. The son answered the door, and my friend was shocked to see the son's face all distorted. My friend had encountered a lot of persons who had demons, and he had helped free them from these evil spirits. He recognized the distortion as demonic and confronted the demon and cast it out, and the son was healed.

My friend returned home that afternoon to find that a sweet perfume filled his house. He went into the bedroom, and the scent was there. He went into the kitchen, and the scent filled that room. He found his wife on her knees, praying and crying. They could only conclude that the perfume was the presence of the Lord, apparently in response for having liberated the pastor's son from the demon.

This intercessor and his wife, who prayed much, told me that one morning as he was getting out of bed to pray, he saw the feet and legs of a tall person standing beside his bed. He assumed the person was an angel standing guard over him. I asked him what the angel looked like, and he could not answer me because he had been afraid to look up at the person. I asked when was the last time he had seen this angel. He said, "Oh, a couple of days ago, he shows up often."

I conclude that God sends messengers to protect intercessors if they need it.

The other person I interviewed, a woman who is known to be an effective intercessor, also gave me an afternoon to listen to her. The missionary told me that God was always bringing people to her to be saved. She was very fruitful in evangelism.

As I sat in her living room, which had a glass door to a little patio garden, she shared much. Her daughter is married to a pastor. The end of the line of the train station is in Buenos Aires. Poor people from the countryside would put a child on the train to the end of the line. The city of Buenos Aires was stuck with these abandoned children.

The city contacted the pastor, asking for the church to care for some of the orphans. The city agreed to provide the church with food and electricity to care for these orphans. It was a very poor church. Soon, according to this lady, the city stopped providing for these children, and the church could not afford to care for them.

The woman told me that her daughter had visited her in that very room to tell her that they were going to have to send the children out into the street. They both were crying about the terrible situation of these children that the church could not care for. While talking to me, she pointed to the patio glass door and said that as they were crying, an angel appeared in the patio with a sword in its hand and struck a stretched-out pose. A voice rumbled through the glass door, saying in Spanish, "Este negocio es mío, y yo cuidaré de ello.—This is a project committed to my charge, and I will take care of it."

From that time on, finances gradually came in from the congregation to enable them to keep the orphanage open.

CARACAS, VENEZUELA

In Venezuela, Navigator missionaries had heard of the results of the five days of listening to God, and some months later, they contacted Rusty and me to come there and do the same. They, too, were struggling. We arrived there a couple of days early to get to know them. I brought with me a man from California. Vincente, whom I was discipling, was an intercessor and spoke Spanish. (We did all these retreats in Spanish. Both Rusty and I had lived and labored in Spain and so were fluent in Spanish.)

As we were getting acquainted, some shared that there was evil spirit activity that concerned them. They had heard that there were some witches who wanted to make pastors and missionaries become disgraced through sexual encounters. One of these missionaries discovered that a witch was following him, looking for opportunities. This concerned them.

We stayed with one of the missionary couples who had two teenage children. At night one of them would see in his bedroom a demon hanging onto the bedroom walls. No one knew how to solve these things.

The first morning of our prayer and listening-to-God meetings, God led us to Psalm 91:1–2: "He who dwells in the shelter of the Most High Will abide in the shadow of the Almighty. I will say to the LORD, 'My refuge and my fortress, My God, in whom I trust!'"

We realized that we needed spiritual protection. They would send the kids off to school during the day as we were praying and were concerned about them and ourselves.

We saw God as our refuge and fortress. We decided to, in prayer, have each one of us declare to God that we were entering into His fortress. We each named our family members who were not present and declared that we were bringing them into that fortress of God's protection, wherever they were.

During the next five days of prayer, we were confident that God was protecting all of us and our family members. We had some great times of listening to God and of prayer. One of us was very touched by this passage: "There was reclining on Jesus' bosom one of His disciples, whom Jesus loved" John 13:23. As we discussed this idea, we decided to make a pact together that each day after this, as we went to our normal residences, we would live by the following commitment. It was very meaningful for all of us. We printed out this decision on paper and put them in wood frames for each of us to take home and put on our desks as a reminder of our commitment. We wrote:

We affirm together that by virtue of the anointing and empowering of God, from this day forward we will live in a new way—that we will rest our heads continually upon the breast of Jesus—and be listeners before doing. We will listen to His voice as the central focus behind all that we say and do. We agree together that YOU GOD are going to do this by the irresistible grace of Christ.

Isaiah 40:11

Sam and Carrie Clark, Harry and Robin Durgin, Ken Guynn, Jack Blanch, Vince Martinez and Rusty Rustenbach

CARACAS, VENEZUELA—FEBRUARY 3, 1999

Now, seventeen years later, this plaque sits on our living room.

When Vincente and I returned home to California, our wives had an interesting tale to tell us. After we had caught our flights for Caracas, both Joann and Vincente's wife experienced unusual attacks of fear in their homes. At night Vincente's wife had a strong fear of someone breaking down their front door and assaulting her. Joann had a fear, too, but of a different type.

On Monday, when we were in Venezuela and spiritually entering the fortress of God, bringing our family members with us, at that time both wives in California were freed from their fears. We concluded that the enemy had been attacking them but that this fortress protection was effective.

In each place where we went, we learned something different about God, ourselves, and the enemy.

SANTIAGO DE COMPOSTELA, SPAIN (OUR FORMER HOME FOR TWELVE YEARS)

I had written to my Spanish friends in Santiago, explaining what we had done in other cities to see if they would like to do the same. They responded positively, so I reserved seven to eight days for a five-day prayer and listening session. In my planning, I made serious error. I was thinking American. I was going to where we had led many people to Christ who loved us and whom we loved. I had planned without counting on Spanish custom. The plan would not work as it had previously. We had reserved a house in the country where we could be alone and pray. In American meetings, if a meeting is in session, new arrivals sit in the back, waiting for break time. In Spain, what the custom is that when a new person arrives during a meeting, the meeting stops, and we all greet, hug, and kiss the new person or persons.

The house for our meeting was geographically in the center of our friendships. People who were not invited to the meeting would come to greet me. It was great for renewing friendships, but it was impossible to have over an hour of meeting without being interrupted.

My second mistake was not remembering that Spaniards are very independent. They don't follow schedules, and they don't follow the "leader's" agenda. When I said we would not be discussing topics but would just listen to God and follow His lead, someone would stand up and announce that he or she wanted to talk about some issue on his or her mind. In Spain, you cannot tell people to sit down and be quiet. It is just not right.

So what was the result of these five days? Nothing of what I had planned. People did not want to hear from God. They wanted to hear from each other. I am not sure what anyone else learned, but I learned two or three things. Was this God's plan?

I was reminded that friendship is more important than meetings; that Spaniards all have their own opinions and want and need to be heard; and that God had used in a special way a message I gave three or four years prior.

One of the couples who visited me told this story. Just before leaving Santiago years earlier, I had been invited to give a message in church. I spoke on the necessity of having a daily time with God to hear His voice.

The wife of an elder of the church was deeply touched. She recounted how she returned home and decided to spend an hour a day reading the Bible and praying. She had the task, among other things, of milking the cows before breakfast and then preparing breakfast for her husband and son. She normally got up at 5:00 a.m. to do her chores but decided to get up at 4:00 a.m. each day to have her hour with God. She told me that her life changed so much that her husband's life was transformed, too.

He now took up his part of the story, telling that he had a special gift of knowing how to treat people's ailments. Keep in mind that this was a very rural area without much access to medical facilities. He began to travel around, visiting the farmhouses and helping any way he could. In the process he was sharing Christ, and many people were responding. This was his open door for evangelism. They both were just beaming as how their lives had been changed through the application of one simple message. This is very precious to me, and what a blessing it was to come home to Joann and share their testimony.

MADRID, SPAIN

A couple of years later, the country leader and I organized a five-day listening conference in Madrid. Joann and I brought a lady from Texas, and other laborers from Spain joined us in Madrid. People had a mind to listen, read, and pray and were of one mind and heart.

In these times together, it is difficult to evaluate what God has done in each heart. They turn out to be life-changing times.

Sometimes something national happens. The one thing that I recall is that one day, the Lord led us to divide into two groups of four or five and pray for the city and nation. One group of us (my group) went to the palace to pray, and the other group went to the congressional buildings.

Because sometimes there were terrorist activities, it was not announced that on that day, the new government was being installed in the parliament buildings. The other prayer group was surprised to see helicopters flying overhead as they walked around the grounds, praying for the nation.

On Monday, the papers stated that the transition had occurred that day, and that a rare peace and cooperation between the parties had occurred during the event. It had a national impact.

In summary, the weekends of fasting and prayer would be valuable for most people. The five days of prayer and listening to God are more for ministry leaders to draw their teams near to God.

13

Influencing Others to Pray

If praying is so effective, how can we have a significant impact? How can you have a greater impact?

Overcoming Personal Obstacles

What are the obstacles to you having a significant impact? If you don't pray, and if you have no clear vision of what God would like to accomplish through you, not much will happen. Here are four things that will keep you from having a positive impact on the world around you.

1. Perhaps you have no vision for what God could do through you. You are unmotivated. How did Jesus motivate people?

   After Jesus rose from the dead, seven of the apostles were headed north toward Galilee. Peter said he was going fishing. The other six were sidetracked by him and went fishing too. All that night they caught nothing. "For without me you can do nothing." Sometimes Jesus blocks our efforts to teach us something. He emphasized this by saying to them that morning, "You don't have any fish, do you?" They admitted, "No."

Then He contrasted their useless efforts with His resource. He promised them that if they cast the net on the other side of the boat, they would catch fish.

They caught more than they could pull in! They then recognized that Jesus gave them abundant success. It was a huge catch without breaking the net. See John chapter 21.

Can you see any parallels for your own life? Could this incident motivate you?

2. Being worn out is an obstacle. Are you worn out through sickness, discouragement, worry, or long hours of work?

   Elijah was discouraged, worn out, and afraid. He was running from the threats of Jezebel. Exhausted, he lay down and slept. An angel showed up and baked hot, fresh bread and gave him water. The angel did this twice, and it gave Elijah strength to walk for forty days without stopping.

   Is there anything for you here? Could God bring a resource to rejuvenate you?

3. Do you have a life without margins? Sometimes people get into a situation where they have no choice but to work exceptionally long hours. Single parents often fall into this category. We don't stop breathing because we are busy. Prayer is like breathing. You can always mentally send up a prayer to God. Ask God for free time for your mind, even though your hands might be busy or you are walking somewhere. God will help.

   Others get into this situation through their own choice or through bad decisions.

   In the Old Testament, in a battle, a man was assigned to guard a prisoner and was told there would be a heavy penalty if he escaped. The prisoner then escaped. "While your servant was busy here and there, he was gone." And the king of Israel said to him, "So shall your judgment be; *you yourself have decided it.*" 1 Kings 20:40.

You are responsible for the decisions that have left you with no space in your life for prayer. Do you blame God for your predicament? I have been in this situation, and by beseeching God to help me get out of a situation that I had put myself in, I found that God is compassionate and has come to my rescue. Consider the illustration at the end of chapter 6 of this book, "The Rest of Believing," where God rescued a couple.

4. Here is some advice when encountering enemy spiritual opposition.

   Paul says that we should put on our spiritual armor to be able to withstand spiritual opposition. Ephesians 6:1–17. This resource is available for you. Review chapter 10, "Defeating Demonic Forces."

Establish a Group of Two to Four Committed Prayer Partners—by phone or Skype, or in person.

If we want to have a long-term impact, we cannot go it alone. As Elijah listened to the voice of God in the desert, he was introduced to a partner in his mission. God guided him to Elisha. They became companions in serving God—two prophets serving together.

As we think about serving God in prayer and becoming His change agents, it is not normally a mission of loners but of partners. Jesus gives us special encouragement to pray together.

> Again I say to you, that if two of you agree on earth about anything that they may ask, it shall be done for them by My Father who is in heaven. For where two or three have gathered together in My name, I am there in their midst.
> Matthew 18:19–20.

The Lord's Prayer begins with "*Our* Father," not "*My* Father," making it a prayer of community.

To have a sustained impact, we need to be bonded together in small groups. You will need to recruit two or three or more who will be committed to this ministry of being God's change agents. Your first prayer in making a sustained impact might be, **"Lord, give me one or two partners in this intercession."**

In this book, we learned that a key to answered prayer is to pray in the will of God, for what God wants. I think the above prayer falls into that category.

Being together physically to pray is probably the most effective way, but using Skype and seeing each other on the screen is a close second. Maybe you can do a Skype conference call and get two to four people on the same call.

A scheduled weekly phone call can also do the trick. I know a person who prays weekly with her friend for half an hour.

As a group of two to four, you should try asking God together what you should be praying for in addition to the Prayer of Faith and Vision at the end of this chapter. There may be something for your workplace, neighborhood, church, or city that God would lead your group to agree on. He will guide you and give you faith for the thing that He will put on your hearts. Don't jump to conclusions. Wait on God and believe He will show you what your particular group should be believing God for. I write down prayers that I am praying, and I record the answers. These are encouraging to read. I usually put down the starting date for my prayer request.

Ministry Prayer Partners

Most mission organizations require their missionaries to establish two to three support groups before they are allowed to go overseas. They are

1. a funding support group to finance them;
2. a prayer support group to allow them to have a successful ministry; and
3. a personal support group at their home bases to solve a host of personal issues.

Why is the prayer group so important? Because the prayers of believers move the hand of God. Before going overseas, Joann and I had the incredible good fortune of knowing some missionaries who believed that their work would languish unless they had a solid group of praying people backing them.

Often, we witnessed that these prayers would be the cause of finding new solutions and of liberating people from the grasp of Satan. He could not hold them when faced with the power of intercessory prayer.

After recruiting about two hundred prayer partners, we pledged ourselves to keep them informed of our progress or the lack of it. We believed that they were responsible for the progress we made. Many of the same people are still praying for us after forty or fifty years!

To our surprise, when we returned to our homeland, we found that many ministries in the United States lacked sufficient prayer backing. Often the workers here did not perceive the crucial importance of solid prayer backing. We even found that some missionaries also did not perceive the importance of the partnership of these laborers.

In one of the countries that I visited, the missionaries were having an almost imperceptible influence on their nation. It was puzzling to me until I questioned the lead missionary in that country about his prayer team from his home country. I asked him how many committed prayer partners he had. He thought for a minute or two, and then lifted up three fingers on one hand, indicating the number. He obviously had thought he could succeed without prayer partners.

Are you following his example, or have you made a conscious effort to recruit people to back what God has called you to do? Do you want to be significantly successful in honoring Christ? Are you committed to keeping them informed, or is that too much effort for you? I constantly recruit new prayer partners, knowing that I must replenish those who drop off due to a wide variety of reasons. We now have quite a few beyond the original two hundred whom we initially recruited. These people love us and are unbelievable encouragers and backers.

If you, after reading this book, have become convinced that people of faith and love are God's change agents, and if you are convinced that the ministry you are doing is important to God, start recruiting some godly prayer partners who are full of faith. You can keep them informed through e-mail, phone calls, or letters. Do not delay!

Below is a prayer that I use to lift my vision.

A Prayer of Faith and Vision
"God, give us a multitude of men and women of God, people after Your own heart, who will do all Your will; men and women who, while doing whatever You call them to do, will believe You to reproduce more people of this same kind."

There are three parts to this prayer.

1. A prayer for men and women of God who have a testimony like Samuel.

But the servant replied, "**Look, in this town there is a man of God**; he is highly respected, and everything he says comes true. Let's go there now. Perhaps he will tell us what way to take." 1 Samuel 9:6 (NIV)

2. A prayer for people who will do the will of God like Jesus and David.

Jesus said: "But so that the world may know that I love the Father, I do exactly as the Father commanded Me." John 14:31.

God's testimony about David: "After removing Saul, he made David their king. He testified concerning him: 'I have found David son of Jesse, a man after my own heart; he will do everything I want him to do.'" Acts 13:22 (NIV).

3. A petition that out of my life will come generations of people of this same kind.

To help people in intercession, I established a website for ideas and interaction. Please visit this site and, if you like it, recruit others to visit it, too. I hope to post to it monthly. Visit www.facebook.com/godschangeagent.

14

Final Thoughts

This book contains a lifetime of learning about prayer and God Himself. I did not learn these things all at once. God taught me year after year. Perhaps there is some special thing that God has spoken to you about, a chapter about resting or about faith or some other chapter. Return to that chapter that is special for you at this time. Immerse yourself in it to learn what God has for you. Don't rush it. It may take God a year to form some aspect of prayer in your life. Be patient. Become a learner about God and about intercession. But don't just learn; apply.

Jerry White said in his Foreword to this book: "I encourage you to read a chapter and then practice what it teaches. This is not a book to read in one sitting. Like so many classic works on prayer, it should be digested slowly with meditation...and, of course, with prayer."

People who have previewed this manuscript have counseled me to include more illustrations of answered prayer and illustrations of the power of God. Following their advice, a number of illustrations were added to chapter 11. The following is a record with dates of how God worked in one particular person. As you read it, take it as a case study on God working in and through people. Meditate on it and see what God has to say to you from it.

Recorded on July 10, 2016, by Jack Blanch.

John Taylor of England in the following e-mails referred to three messages by me in 1969 while Joann and I were living in England. The following is an excerpt from his e-mail in 2011 so that you get an idea of time frame.

John Taylor's e-mail of March 17, 2011:

The strange thing about your major input into my life, Jack, was that I did not really know you at all on a one-to-one relationship, but your impact was solely down to your messages, and this in just three messages in particular…during my first about 3 or 4 months as a Christian. A person's messages only carry weight in so far as they are living them out in practice. The reason God was able to penetrate my heart so powerfully through your messages was because they were so clearly burdened on your heart and part of your life. So it is not really as simple as just your messages changing my life: it was you yourself, in effect.

I want to get down in print these specific major milestones in my very early spiritual journey which have stayed with me all these years and which I have always wanted to thank you for. In chronological order, the major impacts you have had on my life were (as I say, no. 3 being the big one).

"**A message on Psalm 1**, where you contrasted the man who trusted in the Lord—stable, secure and fruitful—with the unbeliever being blown about like tumbleweed, given at Fred & Sheila Horrox's house (Delacourt Rd, Manchester). God spoke to me so powerfully through this that, even 42 years later, I cannot think of Ps 1 or read it without remembering you and your message as I was sat on that crowded floor of the Horrox's back room one night. It is if it was yesterday.

"**A message** in the same circumstances exactly—the crowded back room of the Horrox's house—**expounding Revelations 5:12** in which you took each attribute listed and spoke on the worthiness of God. Again, I just knew God was speaking to me…

"However, the following is by far and away the main thing I want to thank you for, Jack. **This has changed the whole course of my life and I believe will do until I die**: your message on multiplying disciples given at Bully Cottage, Lake District, near Lake Bassenthwaite at about New Year 1970. I would say God spoke to me more powerfully and clearly through this message than any I have ever heard, before or since. About nine of us sat around while you gave a talk based on **Exodus 1:12**. All I can say is that my heart literally burned within me as I stared into the glowing embers of the fire listening to your vision for multiplying disciples. I did not need anyone to tell me this was *God* speaking to me; I just knew it. I just knew, and could hardly believe it, especially so early on in my Christian life, that right there and then God was giving me *my life's vision*...I am sure my efforts have been meagre and I desperately need more men to help but I try and keep the decks clear for this and do not want to just fill slots in church vacancies. When I do one-to-one work based on this vision, all I can say is that my heart leaps within me in a sense of fulfilment and I just know this is God's will for me...

"I could fill one side of a sheet of paper with the list of men I have offered to help spiritually on a one-to-one basis over the last few years and who have declined my offer. But this does not stop me pointing my life in this direction."

A side note as I write this: I put John and his wife on my prayer list in 2011, and have prayed for them three to four times a week for the past five years. My only input has been to encourage him to read my book *Disciple Making for a New Generation*. The following is probably the result of those prayers. *It shows life transformation and a new success at disciple making.*

His e-mail of July 7, 2016, five years later:

"Thanks for your response to my email. What a privilege to have you pray for me and Margaret—I cannot get my head round this!

> The strange thing is that over the past year or two—from about the time I first got in touch with you, via Jack Garratt—I don't know whether I am imagining this or not, and experience tells us to be cautious in jumping to assumptions that any given set of thoughts is God's guidance, *but it "feels" as if God is doing a new thing in my life: a new sort of freedom, a step forward in my Christian life* which I cannot explain to someone else but it seems very real to me. **It applies both to my internal spiritual life and also my dealings with others, including my ("attempted") disciplemaking. I sometimes feel I am becoming a new person, in a good sense, and that it is God's doing, not explainable by any self-effort on my part but likely to be someone in the background praying for me(?)** So I will never really know whether I am just imagining this or not, but if it is down to someone else's prayers and if that someone is you (or maybe you and others as well?), I am so grateful—in fact, this is a gross understatement.
>
> "I would be grateful for your prayers for Bijaya (pronounced "Bi*zay*"), a Nepalese young Christian I am helping at the moment, who so far God has given me a wonderful relationship with, and also for Mek (pronounced "Make"), a close relative of his but who is a bit more remote than Bijaya, who I am also seeking to help spiritually. I also try and help with their English. Then there is Alex, a more mature Christian I have been helping for a few years. After a long gap in us meeting due to our respective especially busy circumstances over the last nine months, he has just emailed me on how he has missed our one-to-one meetings and is keen to resume, so I am overjoyed at this—I know for sure he is still interested (we are meeting for personal bible study discussion)."

What can we draw out of this? If a person is praying to have an impact of disciple making, God can bring it about even if years pass without you, the prayer, knowing what has been happening.

People Who Have Had a Significant Influence in My Life about Prayer and Faith

Jesus said the first will be last and the last first. I wonder if women who pray will be the first in the Kingdom of God. As I review in my mind people of prayer whom I have known, there are very few men; the overwhelming majority have been women.

- Dawson Trotman
- Warren Myers
- Mrs. Jones, a housewife whom I knew as a teenager in the 1940s. She was a member of our church in Oakland, California.
- Mrs. Peterson, a college class teacher in San Diego, California. Her ministry was prayer. I asked her to take on our ministry as a prayer project. She replied that I did not know what I was asking of her. She did not feel she could take up another ministry. She changed her mind later on and became one of our stalwarts.
- Mrs. Goode, who would get a hotel room in the Billy Graham crusades, isolate herself, and pray day after day, traveling from crusade to crusade. Each crusade lasted about a week. I believe the crusade paid for her hotel. She traveled with me one time from Colorado to California, just the two of us in the car. She spent the entire trip praying out loud as I drove. I arrived in California exhausted from listening to her pray.
- Mrs. Hautamakie in San Diego was a woman of prayer.
- Mrs. Noyes of San Diego
- Home of Peace in Oakland, which housed missionaries going out from the West Coast. I attended a regular ladies' group that prayed for the missionaries who shipped out from there. The group numbered five or six. They brought a stack of prayer letters each time they met, maybe fifty to one hundred letters. The ladies divided them up among themselves beforehand and had all the important requests underlined. They prayed like a well-oiled machine for the entire time, two to three hours—no discussion, just prayer. They were impressive.

- People on our prayer letter list. We recruited people to pray for us at least three times a week, and some of them have told us that pray every day. As I stated a little earlier, we recruited about two hundred of these prayers when we first went overseas. Since then, every time that I spoke in church, I recruited new people to pray. The number has more than tripled over these past years. Many have been praying for us for at least fifty years.
- Cacho in Argentina
- Marité in Spain
- Joe and Pam Holt, retired Navigator staff

These are personal friends of ours. I am sure there are many more whom I should have mentioned. Many of these have gone to Glory.

As we all collaborate together, seeking to bring new power and hope to this generation, I asked myself how I could end this book on an encouraging note. I think I should end it as Jesus ended His final sermon to the five hundred after His resurrection.

He had just given the command to go and make disciples of all nations. He preceded this command with a statement of His heavenly and earthly authority: "All authority has been given to Me in heaven and on earth." Matthew 28:18. Jesus was granted by His Father total authority in heaven above and on Earth beneath. That is why He said about Himself, "To the angel of the church in Philadelphia write: He who is holy, who is true, who has the key of David, **who opens and no one will shut, and who shuts and no one opens**." Revelation 3:7. This is the One who goes before us.

Then, after giving them (us) the command in Matthew 28 to go to the world, He followed it with the promise of His presence to accompany those who engage in this command: "And lo, I am with you always, even to the end of the age." Matthew 28:20.

David expressed this clearly: "For David says of Him, 'I SAW THE LORD ALWAYS IN MY PRESENCE; FOR HE IS AT MY RIGHT HAND, SO

THAT I WILL NOT BE SHAKEN.'" Acts 2:25. Jesus, as we go, wants us to realize He is at our right hand so that we can go with all confidence.

Go with the presence of the resurrected Jesus and pray with this same confidence in Him, my friends!

RESOURCES

These are books that have made a significant impact on me for prayer and faith.

The Bible.

Edwards, Jonathan. *The Life and Diary of David Brainerd.* Peabody, MA: Hendrickson Publishers, 2014.

Finney, Charles G. *Autobiography of Charles G. Finney.* Old Tappan, NJ: Fleming H. Revel Co., 1876. (About five hundred thousand came to Christ in New England, 1830–1870).

Finney, Charles G. *Principles of Revival.* Minneapolis, MN: Bethany House Publishers, 1987.

Fraser, J. O. *Behind the Ranges.* Chicago, IL: Moody Press, 1964. (He influenced a whole people group in China).

Geegh, Mary. *God Guides.* Wausau, WI: Color Vision Printing, 2000.

Hallesby, O. *Prayer.* Minneapolis, MN: Augsburg Fortress, 1994.

Hastings, Horace Lorenzo. *Ebenezers (Or Records of Prevailing Prayer).* London: Haughton & Co., 1882.

Miller, Basil. *Praying Hyde.* Grand Rapids, MI: Zondervan Pub., 1943. (He significantly influenced India).

Murray, Andrew. *The Prayer Life.* Pittsburg, PA: Whitaker House, 1981.

Pierson, Arthur. *George Muller of Bristol.* Old Tappan, NJ: Fleming H. Revell Co.

Made in the USA
San Bernardino, CA
27 February 2017